LEVEL UP

Quests to Master Mindset, Overcome Procrastination, and Increase Productivity

A Guide for Writers, Entrepreneurs, and Creatives

by Rochelle Melander

Published 2019 / Dream Keepers Press
Printed in the United States of America
(MOBI) E-ISBN: 978-1-950515-01-1
(EPUB) E-ISBN: ISBN-13: 978-1-950515-00-4
PRINT: ISBN-13: 978-1-950515-03-5

Library of Congress Control Number: 2019903255
Level Up: written by Rochelle Melander
Edited by Amanda Valentine
Layout by Thomas Deeny
Cover Design by James, GoOnWrite.com

Advanced praise for
Level Up: Quests to Master Mindset,
Overcome Procrastination,
and Increase Productivity

Level Up is a rare writing book, one that feels as though it were written just for me. By breaking down the writing process into bite-sized tasks or "quests," it has given me a fresh new set of tools to nibble my way to a strong writing rhythm. It's not only fired up my desire to get to work on my writing projects, but provides a mountain of fuel to keep it burning for a long time. If you've been frustrated in your inability to make progress on your book, your articles, or your business, this is the book you've been waiting for.

– Margaret Terrian Rode, coach, consultant
and tech Sherpa, author of *Storytelling for
Small Business: Creating and Growing an
Authentic Business Through the Power of Story*

In a word: WOW. My reviewer's copy is covered with margin notes! Whether you write for a living, have a creative project you want to undertake (like that long-awaited novel, perhaps), or write as part of your job, Rochelle has made your work easier. Each short, insightful lesson includes specific strategies to take your writing goals, whether personal or professional, from "wanna-do"s to "have-dones." As a longtime freelancer of 20+ years, I have to say it's also worth a look if you're need of inspiration or a new approach when your motivation flags.

– Kelly K. James, author of
*Six-Figure Freelancing, Second Edition:
The Writer's Guide to Making More Money*

Level Up is like the classic "Choose Your Own Adventure" book I grew up with—but instead of going on an adventure, you get to improve your creative work, which is a useful twist on a familiar topic. Most importantly—it's FUN! And who can't use some more fun when they're struggling to write, edit, and create something that changes the world. Pick up a copy of *Level Up* and kick your creativity into high gear. I LOVE this book!

– Phil Gerbyshak, speaker, trainer and author
of 6 books, including *Digital Selling Strategies*

Rochelle Melander's clear, concise prose will be a useful guide to anyone who wants to create. She draws on her years of experience coaching writers, and juggling the demands of her own family and career. She knows the obstacles and she provides step-by-step methods to help you overcome them. If you follow her advice, you will definitely level up.

— Jane Kelley, author of many
middle grade novels, including
The Desperate Adventures of Zeno and Alya

With more than a decade's experience in coaching writers to overcome their blocks, Rochelle shares proven methods in this book to enjoy and THRIVE with writing projects. And, her writing is a pleasure to read. Enjoy and implement this worthwhile book!

— George Kao, author of *Joyful Productivity*

Writing is life. Life is writing. To do either well, we must learn to do both. Rochelle Melander's insightful challenges for "leveling up" are ultimately about encouraging all of us to be all that we can be—as both writers and humans.

— K.M. Weiland, *Creating Character Arcs*

There are no cheat codes in *Level Up*. What you'll find are a ton of practical quests designed to help any writer develop confidence and productivity skills to get a project from dream to done. *Level Up* is going on my keeper shelf!

— Elizabeth Cole, *Secrets of the Zodiac* series

While *Level Up*'s personalized exercises will appeal to anyone who wants to increase their productivity, its fun and intuitive exercises especially spoke to the writer in me. Reading it was like having a personal writing coach by my side! This choose-your-own-adventure-style book teaches creatives how to level up from time wasters to time masters.

— Jessica Lourey, TEDx presenter and author
of *Rewrite Your Life: Discover Your Truth
Through the Healing Power of Fiction*

Writing can be a lonely business, but it doesn't have to be. If you've ever wished you had someone to walk you through the process of doing the creative work you want to accomplish, let Rochelle Melander guide you.

> – Lori Rader-Day, Edgar® Award-
> nominated author of *Under a Dark Sky*

An excellent and engaging way to find what works for each of us as individuals and overcome what's standing in our way. Highly recommended for anyone looking to understand themselves better, set writing goals and find ways to actually meet them.

> – Erica Ruth Neubauer, author of
> *Murder at the Mena House*

Consider Rochelle Melander's *Level Up: Quests to Master Mindset, Overcome Procrastination and Increase Productivity, A Guide for Writers, Entrepreneurs, and Creatives* the more practical, younger cousin of Julia Cameron's *The Artist's Way*. It's a must-read for any writer's bookshelf, and deserves to sit there right along side Anne Lamott's *Bird by Bird* and Natalie Goldberg's *Writing Down the Bones*. Melander, who is both an author and a writing coach, reveals some of her most powerful techniques to help writers and other creatives break through the common challenges they face so that their work becomes more joyful, productive and, ultimately, successful.

> – Jeanette Hurt, author of *Drink Like a Woman*

With the dizzying array of options from which writers and creatives have to choose, Melander's superlative resource breaks through the clutter and offers a systematic, effective, clear—and above all, fun—approach to achieving your creative goals.

> – Dan Maurer, an award-winning Hazelden author.

Level Up is the coach you need to write your own playbook and craft your own success. Brilliant, comprehensive, and life-changing. Start where you are, get this book, and apply even a few pages of its wisdom, and you will win at life, at crafting the vision and the plan to achieve your dreams. *Level Up* is perfect for use in groups to launch their dreams. Re-write, re-start, re-route your life, art, career with this masterful book.

> – Jane Rubietta, Book and Platform
> Coach, international speaker and author
> of *Worry Less So You Can Live More* and
> *The Forgotten Life of Evelyn Lewis.*

Sharpening our focus and embracing productivity will help us to create our best work, but one-size-fits-all writing systems often fall short. Rochelle Melander's approach in *Level Up: Quests to Master Mindset, Overcome Procrastination and Increase Productivity* is unique, supplying optional "quests" to guide creatives in navigating past common internal obstacles that may hamper success. If you are ready to level up your career through self-reflection and the exploration of ideas on how to optimize your own personal writing process, try this book on for size.

– Angela Ackerman, bestselling author,
international speaker, and creative entrepreneur,
author of *The Emotion Thesaurus*

DEDICATION

For Mom and Dad—who taught me to love playing games.

And for Harold, Sam, and Eliana—who encourage me to play every day!

CONTENTS

INTRODUCTION

Got a problem? No doubt someone has the perfect solution and a how-to guide to solve it. The internet is teeming with answers—tips, tools, and tricks to help you fix just about anything.

Many people claim to be experts, and they've created classes, programs, and systems to help people overcome emotional struggles, lose weight, and live better. Search for information on any subject, and you'll find a plethora of articles, books, and classes to help you solve your problem in a few short steps.

As indie publishing has grown into big business, programs have popped up to help people write and publish books and blogs. They all promote a similar message: follow our plan and write your book quickly. Use our proven system and make a six-figure income as a freelance writer. Implement our process and develop a huge following for your blog. The experts touting these programs promise big results—as long as you follow their plan step-by-step.

While some of this advice can be helpful, it's preposterous to think that there's a single road map for writing and publishing a book, making money as a freelancer, or launching a successful blog. Yes, writing and publishing has some rules. Lessons on craft help us create the best possible book, story, or blog post. We can learn tools that make the process of writing less stressful. And it's helpful to learn the basics of getting published, whether we're submitting a blog post, magazine article, or book. But there isn't a single perfect process for writing. Each of us has our own way, with practices and habits that work for us. We just need to discover it.

Teachers and artists David Bayles and Ted Orland, authors of the book *Art and Fear*, say it this way:

> Your work is your guide: a complete, comprehensive, limitless reference book on your work. There is no other such book, and it is yours alone. It functions this way for no one else. Your fingerprints are all over your work, and you alone know how they got there. Your work tells you about your working methods, your discipline, your strengths and weaknesses, your habitual gestures, your willingness to embrace.[1]

Level Up grew out of my frustration with the current cookie-cutter how-to trend. While I believe and teach some best practices for writers, I also know that trying to follow someone else's process can be frustrating. As novelist and psychologist Karen E. Peterson said, "What works for one writer becomes paralyzing for the next."

I've coached writers for more than ten years. My clients often ask me questions like, "When do you write?" or "How do you overcome procrastination?" I've noticed that when I do share my experiences or offer advice, the information rarely helps my clients succeed at becoming more productive writers. Instead of providing a plan, I invite my clients to observe their habits, record their challenges and best practices, and then examine the data. When they treat their life like a science project, they often make exciting new discoveries. They learn from their own life and establish habits that help them ditch distractions and write more.

Level Up presents a series of quests, short adventures that challenge you to investigate your life and habits to discover and use your own best practices.

Who Can Benefit from This Book?

I wrote this book for my clients: writers and entrepreneurs, professionals, and creatives who write as part of their business. Ideas for projects swirl around their brains, but focusing on a single project from beginning to end can be challenging for them. Each struggles with a different part of the process and sometimes faces multiple obstacles as they work a project from start to finish. They worry over which project to choose, wonder if they're good enough to write this book, or get distracted by the demands of life.

Because I primarily work with people on their writing projects, I use the term "writer" when addressing the reader. I also tend to refer to the work in terms of writing and writing projects, including blogs, articles, novels, and nonfiction books.

But you don't have to be a writer racing against a book deadline to benefit from the quests in this book. No matter what your role or project, if you struggle to get things done—this book is for you. Anyone who takes on projects and then feels overwhelmed, gets derailed, or procrastinates can benefit from this book. You might be a project manager at a company, a graphic designer working on your own, or a student trying to keep up with your assignments. This book will help you discover your vision, detect your strengths, focus on your work, overcome obstacles, and accomplish more than you ever thought possible.

How to Use This Book

"Choose Your Own Adventure" books became popular in the early 80s. These books invited readers to participate in creating the story. Written in the second person, the books asked readers to imagine that they were the main character. The reader made the decisions that affected how the story unfolded. In *You are a Genius*, you—the reader and the protagonist—are a genius who whizzes through college and graduate school by the time you're 14, and must choose between designing spaceships and going into business to make a fortune.[2] Each choice brings you to another decision—and a new adventure.

Think of *Level Up* as a "Choose Your Own Adventure" book focused on your creative work and process. The short quests will help you discover your best practices in several areas of your writing life:

- Vision and Plan Your Ideal Writing Life
- Discover and Implement Your Best Practices
- Master Your Mindset
- Ditch Distractions
- Overcome Obstacles

The quests are presented in a more or less sequential order. The first two sections contain quests that are foundational, helping you vision and create your writing life. These quests help you articulate your vision, set goals, and examine and establish the practices that enable you to produce work. The third section, Master Your Mindset, helps you confront your inner critic and transform your relationship with it. The final two sections, Ditch Distractions and Overcome Obstacles, support you in overcoming procrastination and writer's block so that you can focus on your work and increase your productivity.

Because the quests are arranged sequentially, especially in the first two sections, it can be beneficial to work on the quests in order. But not all quests will apply to you. If any quest addresses a topic you don't need or repeats work you've already done, skip it. Like the "Choose Your Own Adventure" books, you get to design your own game.

At the beginning of each section, I've included an annotated list of quests. In addition, I've added an index in the back of the book to help you find quests to support the issue you're struggling with. Take on the quests that help you win your writing game and ditch the rest. As I say to my clients: Do what works for you.

Why Quests?

Every summer, our local indie bookstore has a Find Waldo scavenger hunt. Players pick up a passport from the bookstore and then hunt for Waldo at various local stores. Completed passports are entered into a drawing for prizes. But the real prize is the quest. The year my daughter and I competed, we had great fun searching for Waldo in our neighborhood shops, including a small pet store, a coffee shop, and the bookstore. We enjoyed traipsing from store to store, asking fellow players and shop owners for help finding Waldo. We got hooked by the game, enjoying the adventure. After playing for a few hours, we felt a bit like real detectives, following the clues to find Waldo.

Think back to the last time you played a game. Whether you were playing against the game or another player, you were probably excited about scooping up power-ups, defeating the villains, claiming your treasure, and moving up to the next level. Challenges like National Blog Posting Month, which encourage participants to write a blog post every day for a month, work because they're set up as games. We're much more motivated to achieve something if we're battling against time, competitors, or for a prize.

In Jane McGonigal's book *SuperBetter*, she tells the story of how gaming helped her recover from a head injury. After several months of dealing with the symptoms of a concussion, McGonigal had become frustrated and depressed. Then she had the thought that would transform her life: what if she turned her recovery into a game? She created a secret identity, recruited allies, battled bad guys, and used power-ups. McGonigal shares why being gameful worked for her—and will work for you:

> Being gameful means bringing the psychological strengths you naturally display when you play games—such as optimism, creativity, courage, and determination—to your real life. It means having the curiosity and openness to play with different strategies to discover what works best. It means building up the resilience to tackle tougher and tougher challenges with greater and greater success.[3]

In this book, you'll take on short quests or games to tackle your creative challenges and discover your best practices. You'll also adopt a secret identity, recruit allies, identify villains, and create your own playbook. Because you'll be using a gameful approach to shaping your creative life, doing these quests won't be a chore. Instead, you'll be able to play with possibilities and maybe even have some fun along the way!

Get Your Game Gear

Most games require gear. Football players need special protective gear, like helmets and shoulder pads. Video gamers must have game consuls. Chess players need a board, clock, and timer.

In addition, games require a bit of set up. Football players study their playbook and learn the key maneuvers. Video gamers design their avatar. Chess players claim their color and set up the board.

For these quests, you'll need to get the appropriate gear and set up your life to play. The following tools will help you treat the quests as games, adventures to conquer on the road to developing a productive writing life:

Adopt a Secret Identity

A few years ago, I was out for a walk when I saw a man struggling to clean up after his dog using a ripped poop bag. I happened to have two unused poop bags in my pocket, left over from a morning walk with my dogs. I offered them to him. He looked at me in surprise and said, "Wow. Thank you. How great to meet the Guardian Angel of Poop Baggies." I laughed, happy to have helped.

But his comment got me thinking: how much better would life be if I had a secret identity, like one of my favorite fictional heroes, Buffy the Vampire Slayer. Use your imagination, your favorite superheroes, or online name generators to develop your own secret identity for your work on this book.

Create Your Playbook

Many of the quests in this book require the use of a journal. As you record your habits and reflect on your life in writing, you'll discover your best practices. Think of your journal as your individual game playbook, your unique how-to guide for writing and life. (I will use the terms journal and playbook interchangeably.) You can use your journal to track your progress as you work through this book and move forward on your current project.

Recruit Allies

During National Novel Writing Month, thousands of people aim to write a 50,000-word novel in 30 days. I've participated for over ten years, and still believe that it's the camaraderie with the other participants that makes the month valuable. Instead of simply sweating over a manuscript alone in my office, I can join writing sprints online, visit write-ins at local libraries and coffee shops, and connect with fellow writers on the message boards. We become allies, cheering each other on and offering advice to help each other move forward. When NaNoWriMo ends, I feel more alone.

But it doesn't have to be that way. We can recruit allies to help us succeed in achieving our goals throughout the year. It might be helpful to have a few allies to work through this book with you. If taking on that task before you begin the book sounds too daunting, there's a quest early in the book to help you recruit and connect with allies (see "26. Identify Your Allies" on page 91).

Identify and Battle Villains

For writers, villains are as much the voices in our heads as they are real people who we encounter on the street or online. I've developed a quest (see "27. Name Your Villains" on page 94) to help you identify the villains who threaten to undermine your confidence and courage. But realize that this whole book is about overcoming the villains who hold us back from writing.

Utilize Power-ups

Power-ups are simply the activities that increase our sense of well-being. When we take a walk, get help from a friend, or eat a healthy snack, we are using a power-up to increase our energy. In the Appendix you'll find a list of power-ups (see "Power-up List" on page 237) that are generally helpful to everyone. In addition, Part Two contains a quest called "25. Discover Favorite Power-ups" on page 89 to help you identify and use your favorite power-ups.

Learn the Drills

Every sport has drills that players learn and practice to learn the fundamental skills necessary for playing the game. Players sprint, pass, and balance to develop the agility they need for the game. These drills help coaches see the players' strengths and weaknesses and adjust the plays accordingly.

When it comes to developing a life that supports writing, the quests in this book will help you examine your past, pay attention to your present, and vision your future. Many of the quests use journaling exercises to help you collect information, analyze the data, and figure out what works for you. The exercises use the following key methods to help you understand your habits and imagine new ways of living:

Mind Map

A mind map is a visual way of making lists or recording ideas. This can be a helpful tool for brainstorming writing projects, collecting ideas, gathering memories, and imagining possibilities for your life.

Write your topic or idea in the middle of the page. Radiating from the word, like spokes on a bicycle wheel, note categories of thought that support the topic: stories, images, themes, sensory details, examples, facts, statistics, and so forth. For each category, record your information, stories, and ideas. When you've written down everything you know, you'll have a visual map to help you solve whatever issue you're working on.

Free Write

Don't think about journaling as a traditional writing assignment, with a beginning, middle, and end. Write what comes to your mind, just like when you are brainstorming or talking through an idea with a colleague or friend. When you don't know what to write next, write that down. Repeat ideas as necessary.

List

Lists come easily because we are used to making lists for daily plans and shopping trips. Instead of worrying about writing paragraphs or even complete sentences, list ideas, questions, concerns, or anything else that comes to mind.

Letter

Journaling can feel forced and self-focused. For people opposed to naval-gazing, it can be difficult to write about oneself. Sometimes it is easier to write a letter to someone about our lives. Address your journal entry to someone you respect and admire. You might even choose to write to a favorite historical person or fictional character. What might Benjamin Franklin or Xena the Warrior Princess advise you to do?

Tracker

We live in a world obsessed with tracking. Fitness trackers help wearers count steps and analyze their sleep patterns. Apps like 42Goals and Momentum help users track their habits and focus on a single goal. And bullet journal creators use analog charts to track everything from the books they read to the water they drink. Many of the quests in this book invite you to create a tracker to examine your life and work habits. You can use an analog version like a chart, a computer spreadsheet, or an app to track your habits.

Ready, Set, Go!

Level Up provides an opportunity for you to discover your strengths, helpful habits, and best practices. As you work through this book, you will be dedicating time to taking care of your creative life. And each quest will help you spend time creating the work you care about. May you have a most excellent adventure!

PART ONE: VISION AND PLAN YOUR IDEAL WRITING LIFE

1. Vision Your Epic Wins
Vision your best possible future self and write about what your life will look like when you have accomplished all of your goals.

2. Capture Your Vision Daily
Each morning, write your vision for the day as if you were living your best possible life.

3. Learn from Envy
Use your feelings of envy to explore your desires.

4. Create a Vision Board
Take the dreams and visions that have surfaced in the last three quests and create a vision board.

5. Map Your Assets
Examine your life and determine all of your assets.

6. Assess Your Knowledge
Review your life and list topics you know a lot about.

7. Identify Your Passions
Use a list of questions to explore what you are passionate about.

8. Connect Your Assets
Connect assets, knowledge, and passions to discover new possibilities.

9. Choose Your Project
Assess potential projects and select one to work on.

10. Write Goals that Work
Phrase your goals in a format that will help you achieve them.

11. Play with Goals
Explore three unique ways to try out new goals.

12. Eliminate Conflicting Goals
Examine your life to discover what other goals or tasks might be getting in the way of achieving your goal.

13. Develop a Life Priority List
Create a list of your life's top priorities.

14. Learn to Say No
Identify tasks you don't want to do and practice saying no.

15. Let It Go
Let go of writing projects, work projects, and other tasks that no longer work for you.

16. Examine the Past
Review the past year and evaluate what's working and what needs to change.

17. Make Peace with Your Past
Celebrate successes and let go of regrets.

1. VISION YOUR EPIC WINS

*Be careful what you wish for, because you might not be dreaming
big enough.*

– Dar Williams

When I was a kid, I wished for a crystal ball to tell me what the future
held. But I didn't have access to fancy magical instruments, so I used a
Magic 8-Ball. Remember those? We'd ask the ball a question, shake it,
and then look for the answer: "Reply hazy, try again." or "Yes–definitely."

These days, I'm more interested in creating plans to accomplish my
own visions. But before we can draft the plan—the road map to our
heart's destiny—we need to understand what we desire. I often work
with clients who are overwhelmed by multiple ideas and possibilities for
writing projects. They flit between projects, wondering which one will
be the sure thing or worrying about how to proceed. They come to me,
hoping that I have the ability to tell their fortunes, predicting which path
will lead to gold. Instead, I invite them to dream big, imagining where
they'd like to be in 1, 5, or 10 years. This vision will unearth their dreams,
help them set goals, and create a road map.

In this quest, you will vision your epic wins. You'll write about what
your life will look like when you have accomplished all of your goals.
Psychology professor Sonja Lyubomirsky discovered that writing about
one's *best possible future self* improved moods, health, and ability to set and
achieve goals.[4] When you vision your best possible future self, you'll feel
like you have peeked through a crystal ball. Once you've seen what you
hope the future could look like, you'll be able to plan how to get there.

The Quest

This quest invites you to consider your future life:

> *Imagine yourself [INSERT FUTURE TIME FRAME HERE].
> Everything has gone as well as it possibly could. You have worked
> hard and succeeded at accomplishing all of your goals. Write in the
> present tense about your life. What does it look like?*

When you do the quest, write in the present tense as if everything
you've envisioned has happened. We'd normally write about the future
like this, "I hope by the end of the year to have finished writing my
nonfiction book on garden snakes." For this quest, you'll write about your
goals in this way: "I finished a draft of my nonfiction book. I am celebrat-
ing with my writing group at my favorite taco place." Use as much sensory

detail as possible. After stating that you finished the draft, describe how it felt. Record the details of your celebration. How do the tacos taste?

In the original study, participants wrote about what their lives would be like in five years. Because we're working on plotting a writing life in the here and now, it can be helpful to create a vision that imagines what might happen in the next month, quarter, or year.

Take your game playbook to a coffee shop or park, and spend 10-20 minutes doing this quest. Do the quest four times, in four different places. Each time, imagine a different scenario for your life. Play with wild and crazy possibilities. Or imagine the same scenario in four different ways, trying different writing forms like a list or a personal artist statement.

As you do the quest, pay attention to how you feel. If you feel especially energized and engaged during parts of your writing, note what you are writing about. What plans excite you? If any plans leave you feeling drained, jot that down, too.

Reflect

When you've finished writing all four of your visions, review what you wrote and look for themes.

- What are the 3-5 consistent themes that show up in your vision?
- What activities or plans consistently energized you?
- What goals appeared out of this practice?
- What creative projects showed up?
- What steps do you need to take to achieve your vision?

Game Play Tips

- Think about creative ways you can do this quest: write an acceptance speech for a coveted award, a profile of yourself for a television news show, or an interview for a popular magazine.
- In the original study, participants did this quest four times. I found that the first time I tried this quest, I was so tethered to the present that I could not envision the future. The second time around, my tether was looser. Each try brought bigger dreams. Do the quest at least twice—and leave some time between tries.
- It's important to do this quest away from home. It's hard to see the seeds for your beautiful life when you are staring at piles of dirty dishes or the stacks of unpaid bills. One of the most persistent villains, the inner critic, will use this information to try to derail you: *How can you accomplish anything when you can't even clean your house?* Defeat that villain by getting out of the house. Go to the art museum, a coffee shop, or library and write there. You will be able to dream bigger dreams.

For the Win

The minute you scribble your vision in your journal, you've entered the winner's circle. Just articulating your vision increases positive emotions like hope and optimism. But writing about your best possible life will also make you more likely to participate in activities and connect with people who are part of your vision. Once you've written about your heart's desires, you can take the first small steps toward your goals.

2. CAPTURE YOUR VISION DAILY

Vision is the art of seeing things invisible.

– Jonathan Swift

Martha Beck wrote a column about getting rid of stuff.[5] Since I'd been madly tearing through my house, dumping books and old clothes into bags and setting them in the Goodwill pile, I paid attention. In her article, she raved about how helpful her daily journaling had been. Martha Beck described this journal as a written vision board.[6]

Writing in a Daily Visioning Journal is much like the work you did in "1. Vision Your Epic Wins" on page 20 but shorter and a little easier to do. The Daily Visioning Journal is a very small journal. Each day, we record a few lines about what we'd be doing that day if we were living our ideal life. The practice helps us vision our future in the tiniest bits possible and then reflect on what we notice about our visions. For readers who have already done the "Vision Your Epic Wins" quest, the Daily Visioning Journal reminds us daily of the life we hope to live.

In this quest, each morning you will write your vision in a journal as if you were living your best possible life. After a few weeks, review the journal and consider what kinds of changes you might want to make to your life. Keeping a Daily Visioning Journal about what you wish your day looked like will help you shape your days in small but significant ways.

The Quest
Choose a small journal or notebook, about the size of an index card. (You could also use a stack of index cards!) Set aside 5 minutes each morning to do this quest.

Step One: Write
For the next week or two, write one page as if you were living your ideal life. Consider:

- If you were living your ideal life, what would you be thinking, writing, and doing?
- Who would you connect with?
- Where would you live?
- How would you spend your days?
- Write in the present tense. Use sensory details.

Step Two: Review

After a few weeks of keeping the Daily Visioning Journal, review your journal entries. As you read, pay attention to three things:

- Entries that energize you
- Negative thoughts and feelings that surface when you read
- Themes that emerge

Step Three: Reflect

- When you feel that surge of energy, that's a sign that what you're reading engages you at a deep level. Consider how you can incorporate more of that activity in your daily life. For example, if you feel energized by the idea of spending an entire day writing, then figure out how you can do that even once a month.
- Recurring dreams and plans can also be signs that you want to do something. Think about what goal you might set to help you achieve your dreams. When you have a goal or even an idea of what you might do next, consider the smallest possible step you can take toward your goal and then try it.
- Entries may also trigger negative feelings or thoughts. For example, you might have written about attending a writing conference and sitting with your new friend, a famous author that you've always admired, and the first thought that pops into your head is, *THAT could never happen.* According to Martha Beck, these negative ideas are the clutter we need to clear away. Change your negative thought into either a question or a positive statement. Instead of, *That could never happen,* try: *How could that happen? What would be the first step?* or *I can imagine how fun it will be to meet my favorite author.* If you continue to have difficulty with negative thoughts—and we all do from time to time—try the quests in "Part Three: Master Your Mindset" on page 127.

Game Play Tips

- Write about a variety of aspects of your life, including professional, personal, physical, spiritual, and more.
- The Daily Visioning Journal can be done in conjunction with the quest "1. Vision Your Epic Wins" on page 20 or alone. It doesn't matter which quest is done first.
- If writing in your Daily Visioning Journal every morning doesn't work, try writing each evening. Write as if you've just spent the day doing exactly what you wish or anticipating what you plan to do the next day. It may also be helpful to do this as a gratitude

journal exercise: *I'm grateful that I've been able to finish my fourth painting this year.*

For the Win

The Daily Visioning Journal offers you the practice of writing about how you would be living each day if you were living your ideal life. It keeps your vision real, tangible, and close to you. In time, visioning will turn to practicing—and you'll be doing more of what matters to you each day.

3. LEARN FROM ENVY

A child can teach an adult three things: to be happy for no reason, to always be busy with something, and to know how to demand with all his might that which he desires.

– Paulo Coelho

Have you ever opened your favorite social media feed, read that a friend has scored a great job, fallen for a new love, or published a book—and felt sick with envy? Stop. Take a deep breath and reflect. What can this envy teach you?

Gretchen Rubin, author of *The Happiness Project*, believes that negative emotions serve an important purpose:

> But negative emotions play a very important role in a happy life, because they warn us that something needs to change. When we envy someone, it's a sign that that person has something that we wish we had for ourselves. And that's useful to know.[7]

Most of the time, envy hits out of the blue. We're scrolling through Instagram or paging through an alumni magazine, and happen upon someone's good news. Wham! A wave of sadness and desire rolls through our bodies and we think, *I wish that was me.* Or maybe we're attending a networking event and meet someone who has succeeded at a job we'd once hoped for. However it happens, envy can hit hard and leave us with feelings of regret. On the plus side, that moment of envy can help us figure out how we want to configure our writing life and what we want to create.

This quest offers you the opportunity to dig deeply underneath your envy and mine it for signs of desire.

The Quest
You need your journal and access to your social media feeds to do this quest.

Step One: Identify the Monster
Do you remember when you've felt the green-eyed monster hit you in the gut? Where were you? What were you doing? Make a list of all of the places you've bumped into that monster—social media feeds, networking events, alumni and organization publications and sites, and social events.

For each memory of envy, record the following information:

- The person, event, or news that triggered your feelings of envy. When you see that a friend has published a novel, note what you wish for. Do you want to write a novel? Are you envying his accomplishment or the attention he is receiving?
- How you felt. What does envy feel like for you? What does it stir up? Do you see a friend's successes and immediately criticize yourself? Do you experience feelings of regret or doubt about yourself? Or do you feel desire for the same type of accomplishment?

Step Two: Search for the Monster

If you can't recall the last time you felt envy, delve into your social media sites and search for news of your colleagues' successes. Pay attention to how you feel as you read about your friends, family members, and colleagues—and note when feelings of envy strike. You'll know you're feeling envy when what someone else has accomplished leaves you thinking:

- *I wish I'd done that.*
- *I'd love to be doing that.*
- *How did she get to do that?*

Again, each time envy strikes, record:

- The person, event, or news that triggered your feelings of envy.
- How you are feeling.

Step Three: Reflect

Reflect on what you learned. Note what the information you've gathered tells you about:

- What you'd like your life to look like (where you live, who you connect with, how you move through your days).
- What creative projects you work on or wish you could work on.
- Any other desires that popped up while you observed the success of others.

Game Play Tips

- If you have difficulty remembering when you felt envy, review old journal entries.
- Envy can be both a teacher and a villain. To look at more villains and how they affect your creative life, do see "27. Name Your Villains" on page 94.
- Take care of yourself. Digging into negative feelings does not feel good. (No kidding!) But it can be a helpful teacher. Take time to comfort and care for yourself after experiencing feelings of regret or doubt. Do a power-up (see "25. Discover Favorite Power-ups" on page 89). Or review your accomplishments and experiences and remind yourself of their value. Try the quests "5. Map Your Assets" on page 32 to review the good things in your life, "22. Recognize Your Strengths" on page 80 to note your best habits, or "41. Adopt a Positive Mantra" on page 136 to help you reframe negative thoughts.
- Remember that everything you have done and survived has made you who you are. You'll be able to take the lessons you've learned and the crazy experiences you've had and write one heck of a book!

For the Win

You're one step closer to understanding just what you want your creative life to look like and what sorts of projects you'd like to complete. Yay you!

4. CREATE A VISION BOARD

The most pathetic person in the world is someone who has sight but no vision.

– Helen Keller

Every year, I create a vision board on a large bulletin board in my office. On it, I place words and images that help me see what I would like to create in the next year. This year, I made several vision boards and placed them around my house and in my journal, so that my vision can be constantly in front of me. Now when I wake up, the first thing I see is a vision board filled with photos of writing retreats and children's books, reminding me to put writing first each day.

Our environment affects how we feel and what we do. Psychologists call this *priming*. Some of the most interesting studies on priming have to do with how marketers influence customers. In one study, a grocery store played stereotypically German and French music on alternate days.[8] The researchers discovered that the type of music influenced purchases: the German music resulted in people purchasing more German wine while the French music led to people buying more French wine. When surveyed afterwards, the participants did not know that the music had influenced their choices.

As a coach, I've encouraged clients to use their environment to support them in accomplishing their goals. A client who wanted to exercise first thing in the morning set out her workout clothes right next to her bed. A writer encouraged himself to capture his best ideas each day by setting his notebook and pen next to his place at the breakfast table. An artist carried around a sketchbook and pens in her purse so that she'd always be ready to capture images. A vision board can be another way to keep your vision in front of you throughout your day—priming you to take small steps toward your vision.

In this quest, you will take the visions you've worked on in the past several quests and create a vision board.

The Quest

Vision boards can be done with physical items like a poster board and photos from magazines or with your computer or tablet.

Step One: Review

Before you begin, review the visions you created for the past quests—"1. Vision Your Epic Wins" on page 20, "2. Capture Your Vision Daily" on page 23, and "3. Learn from Envy" on page 26. Consider what parts of these visions you want to accomplish in the next year and make a list of 5-10 practices (eating better, meditating) or goals (writing a memoir, learning how to write poetry) that you want to focus on this year. If you're not sure what you want to accomplish this year, you might want to do some of the other quests in this section, such as "7. Identify Your Passions" on page 38, "9. Choose Your Project" on page 42, or "11. Play with Goals" on page 47, and then come back to this quest.

Step Two: Gather Materials

PHYSICAL

You'll need a poster board, bulletin board, cardstock, or some other surface to display your vision. Choose whatever size works for you. A large poster board or bulletin board provides ample room but a small vision board that can be tucked in a calendar or journal can be equally inspiring and helpful.

Next, gather magazines, junk mail, old cards, buttons, ribbons, and any other images that may represent your vision. Search for photos online or create mock-ups of your future book covers and print them for use on your board. Collect positive sayings from magazines and cards to add to your vision board or write positive words or quotes on index cards or cardstock. Some people add trinkets to their vision board—feathers, buttons, charms, and other items that reflect who they hope to become. Finally, you'll need something to attach your visions to your board—glue, tape, or push pins.

VIRTUAL

For people who love to play with online tools, virtual vision boards can be fun and just as helpful. There are numerous vision board apps available through your favorite App store but you don't need to buy something special to make your vision board work. Create a vision board on Pinterest with images that represent your goals. Or use a graphic tool like Canva to make a vision board. On your own computer, you can create collages with Word, Pages, or Adobe Photoshop.

Once you've chosen a tool, find or create images to add to your vision board. CreativeCommons holds over a billion works, and you can discover photos of just about anything on the site. The Library of Congress also has millions of images that you are free to use. Canva and other graphic design tools work well for mocking up book covers. Tools like Insta-Quote and Quote Maker are helpful for capturing your word of the year or favorite quotes. Apps like WordArt and Wordle allow you to make collages of your goals. Upload your vision statement or a list of the things you want to do this year, and watch the application turn it into a visual representation of your dreams.

Step Three: Play!

Set aside at least two hours to create your vision board. Review your vision statements, your goals, and any other journaling information you have. Choose a list of 5-10 items you would like to accomplish in the next year, then play with the materials you've gathered to create a visually inspiring version of your vision.

Step Four: Display!

Display your vision board in a place where you can see it every day, either on your computer, tablet, or smart phone or in person. If your board is a physical object, take a photo of it so that you can use it as wallpaper on your computer or phone.

Game Play Tips

- Your vision board is visual and will be largely composed of images. But you can also add words, positive mantras, or quotes to help you move forward with your goals.
- Create a vision playlist of favorite songs to listen to while you're working on your vision board and throughout the year.
- Consider how you might incorporate your secret identity on your vision board. Maybe if you're the Idea Ninja, you'll post an image that reminds you how you'll gather and use these ideas through-out the year to achieve your goals.
- Change it up! As you achieve the goals on your board or change your mind about other visions, revise your board! Glue new photos over the old ones or add new quotes. Keep it fresh and active, like you!

For the Win

We do what's in front of us. Vision boards work because they remind us of our goals in a very tangible way. This small tool will help you move forward with your goals.

5. MAP YOUR ASSETS

When we recognize and appreciate our assets, we transform our thinking. Instead of seeing needs and deficiencies, we see gifts and strengths. We transform negatives into positives. We see our cup as half-full.

– Luther Snow

When financial planners talk about assets, they usually mean money and material stuff, like land, houses, horses, and jewelry. While economic assets are essential—hey, we've got to eat—our other assets can help us create books, businesses, and articles that earn money, too.

Between gigs as an actress, Alice Wilson spent years working as a model for art classes, which taught her how to stay still for hours. When she encountered living statues in Chicago and Las Vegas, she had an idea. She put her unique talents as a performer and crafter together and constructed a costume for a statue of Willy Wonka. Since then, she's become known as Milwaukee's first living statue and created unique costumes for performances as a steampunk nanny, Puck, Benjamin Franklin, and more. Wilson is a perfect example of how uncovering and combining unique assets can lead to a career.

This quest will help you examine your life and determine your assets.

The Quest

Set aside at least an hour to do this quest. I use mind mapping to collect my assets, but you can also create a series of lists. Both of these journaling tools are discussed in "Introduction" on page 11. Look at each category and brainstorm your assets:

Physical Assets

Things you can touch, see, or feel. This might include your computer, books, or your large collection of pens! I'd also include the assets you've collected on your computer or online, like your half-written novel or your boards on Pinterest.

Individual Assets

List your talents, experiences, skills, preferences, and everything you wonder about. This might include your skill of explaining difficult topics, interest in how copper is mined, or ability to catch typographical errors that everyone else has missed!

Associations

Note who you know and who you hang out with. This might be a list of editors, agents, and other writers as well as your colleagues in other fields. Also add any groups or networks you belong to, both professional and social. You might list your exercise buddies at the gym, the professional networking group you meet with, and your neighborhood book group. Don't forget your online buddies—the people you know through LinkedIn, Twitter, Facebook, and more.

Institutions

Make a list of the businesses, public agencies, and nonprofit institutions that you connect with regularly. Include the schools you attended and the places you've done work for (whether volunteer or for a fee).

Economic Assets

Record what you earn and what you have saved, including any investments or property that you didn't list in physical assets. Include anything you can do for money (Babysit? Cook? Write!).

Other Assets

Have I missed a category or two? Add them and the assets that belong to the categories.

Game Play Tips

If you come to the end of this quest and feel like you're missing something, try looking for assets in one of these places:

- Review your previous jobs, even the ones that you hated. What assets did you cultivate in those jobs that you can use now? (For example, when I was a minister, I preached every week. In my current work, that translates as public speaking.)
- List any unusual, crazy, or rare skills you have. Perhaps you make candy or sausage for holiday gifts. Or maybe you have the rare talent of finding the perfect Halloween costume. Own it and list it!
- How do your secret identity or your nicknames reflect your assets?
- If you explore all of these paths and still feel like something's missing, talk to a close friend. What assets do they see in you? What connections do they know about that you've overlooked?
- Let the list sit for a day or two. I'm guessing you'll think of even more assets as you're showering, cleaning, or exercising.

For the Win

Every time I create an asset map, I experience an overwhelming sense of gratitude—I am richer than I ever thought possible. Once you've finished your asset map, take a moment to appreciate your many riches. Wow!

6. ASSESS YOUR KNOWLEDGE

Knowing yourself is the beginning of all wisdom.

– Aristotle

The popular radio show *Whad'ya Know?*, hosted by Michael Feldman, began each show with Feldman shouting, "Whad'ya know?" and the audience responding, "Not much, you?" The show quizzed guests on topics in six categories, including current events, people, places, things you should have learned in school (had you been paying attention), science, and odds and ends. When I played along at home, I was often surprised by how much I knew in categories I thought I knew nothing about.

It's amazing what information we soak up over a lifetime of reading books, taking care of business, and talking with others. My clients tend to underestimate what they know and how they can use their knowledge to create blog posts, articles, and books.

In this quest, you will examine your life and create a list of the topics you know a lot about. This information will support you in choosing topics for your writing or other creative projects.

The Quest

Review your life and what you know using the following categories. You might collect the information in a mind map or list, either on paper or in a digital device. As you list what you know in each of the categories, pay attention to how you feel. If you feel energized by any topic, that's important information. Place a star next to those topics.

Academic Training

The information you learned in school or in any other academic training setting.

Professional Training

The information you learned to do your profession. Some of this you learned in a formal school setting, some you learned during job-specific professional training, and some you learned on the job from mentors and colleagues.

Specialized Training or Knowledge

This is highly specific information that you learned either for work or life—maybe blacksmithing, crocheting, how to make hard candy, or operate certain types of machinery.

Professional Experience

This is information you learned while working at your profession. This differs from professional training in that you probably didn't learn this from your teachers, mentors, or supervisors. It can be as vastly different as how to network, the best methods for handling difficult clients, or how to change the toner in the copy machine. Some of this might be stuff you wish you'd never learned, like "how to work with a difficult boss" or "dealing with sexism in the workplace."

Personal Experience

This is stuff you know because you experienced it in your own life. It could be about a life transition, like becoming a parent or moving to a new city; it could be about a trip you took or an illness you suffer from or overcame.

Interests and Curiosities

In this space you can put anything that you are interested in or curious about. These might be the subjects that you take workshops on at conferences or the questions that keep you up at night. You might notice that you check out these sections in the bookstore or library. Or maybe you search out chat rooms or websites on these topics.

Idiosyncrasies

These are odd or quirky topics, so unusual that people rarely write books or hold conferences about them. You seek out information on this topic even though you're slightly embarrassed to admit it.

Collections

The stuff you collect, whether it's clown dolls, baseball cards, aphorisms, or alternative music. This also includes the experiences, artifacts, and souvenirs you've paid money to see or own. This will give you a clue as to what is truly important to you.

Game Play Tips

- You might need more than one sitting to complete these lists. After completing your initial draft, set aside the lists. Over the week or two that follows, new areas of knowledge will occur to you. Add them to the list.
- Review old journals, books, and calendars for information you might be missing. Maybe you forgot about that workshop you attended on workplace bullying.
- Ask friends, colleagues, and coworkers about what kinds of information they turn to you for and what they value about you in the workplace.

For the Win

We live in a world that respects higher education and honors it with jobs. But this quest reminds us that we learn in many ways—and that wisdom never leaves us. We can take that experience and information and turn it into books and more.

7. IDENTIFY YOUR PASSIONS

I have no special talents. I am only passionately curious.

– Albert Einstein

We can have a stellar education and the gift of experience, but what we've studied and worked with much of our lives might leave us feeling bored. That's not uncommon. Most of us don't work in a single job or field for our entire lives. For that reason, when we evaluate our assets, we also need to consider what we are passionate about.

In my book *Write-A-Thon*, I wrote about children's writer and poet Ralph Fletcher[9] who asks his readers to consider their *fierce wonderings* and *bottomless questions*. At a writing workshop, one of my students had done just that. We were writing noisy poetry, and she chose to write about a cat. "I'm obsessed with cats," she announced. As she wrote her poem, she told me several important facts about cats. "You know they can't taste sweet things. They'll eat ice cream, but just because it's milky." As she chattered about cats, I could see how her passion had inspired her to learn as much as she could about cats. All of these facts exploded into a poem.

Passion drives our curiosity. In this quest, you'll consider what you are passionate about.

The Quest

Brainstorm answers to the following questions. If you need more information, review the lists you developed in the last two quests.

- What are you absolutely passionate about?
- What gets you up in the morning?
- What questions or ideas keep you up in the middle of the night?
- What will you work on even if you're sick or tired?
- What images catch your eye at museums, in books, or while driving?
- What topics are you so passionate about that if all your supplies burned up, you'd pay money to replace them?
- What do you love to talk about at parties or networking events?
- What problems or worries do you fantasize about solving?
- What do you buy, attend, or seek out regularly, no matter what else is going on in your life?
- What books or magazines do you seek out at a library or bookstore?
- What jobs, interests, or ideas do you like reading or watching movies about?

- Sometimes our passions get lost in the past. Remember what you loved when you were 10 and free to explore anything. Does thinking about any of these ideas or activities energize you?

Game Play Tips

- If you get stuck, take a look at your collections of books, experiences, and things—do any of these reveal your passions?
- You can also wake sleeping passions by visiting a library, bookstore, museum, or second hand store and wandering around until something piques your curiosity.
- Once you've finished your first try at this list, let it rest. Revisit it in a few days or a week. More ideas will come to you.

For the Win

Many artists recall that their parents advised them to stay away from "the business" at all costs. And by "the business" they meant the arts—acting, singing, painting, or writing. No doubt that warning came out of fear for their security and happiness.

Passions may not always be practical. But because we're willing to work harder for what we love, passions can lead to paychecks. And even if they don't, we'll be happier working on projects that fuel our heart's desires!

8. CONNECT YOUR ASSETS

Eventually everything connects—people, ideas, objects.
— Charles Eames

When our book group meets, everyone brings a dish to add to the table. We often don't plan what we're going to bring but somehow it all works out. (Okay, often we have five desserts, but no one sees that as a problem!) And even with the abundance of desserts, our combined offerings usually make a meal.

When we evaluate our assets individually, they may not look like much. But when we combine our assets, we can find unique ways to use them. For example, I'm tempted to dismiss my short stint as a trainer at the Y. But when I combine that with my love of exercise, my connection to local trainers, and my writing skills—I've discovered a whole new field to write about.

If you've been working through these quests in order, you now have the following lists:

- assets
- knowledge
- passions

In this quest, you will play with combining your assets, knowledge, and passions to create unique and fun opportunities.

The Quest
In Luther Snow's book, *The Power of Asset Mapping*[10], he teaches a simple asset mapping process that works well for groups. I've adapted it here for individual use.

Step One: Name your Assets, Knowledge, and Passions
Remember that you worked with various kinds of assets and knowledge in quests "5. Map Your Assets" on page 32, "6. Assess Your Knowledge" on page 35, and "7. Identify Your Passions" on page 38; those lists will be helpful in this step of the quest. Use a stack of index cards or a pad of sticky notes or other small sheets of paper. Transfer each asset from your list to a single note card or piece of paper. So you might have cards that read: "marathon runner," "avid reader," or "Art Museum Membership."

Step Two: Play with Your Cards!
Combine the cards in interesting ways to create actions that use two or more assets, knowledge, or passions. Don't judge or discard combinations because you cannot see how they'd work in the real world. Just let the cards speak. Sometimes the oddest combinations result in brilliant ideas. The actions you design might be a writing project, art installation, event, class, performance, or just about anything else you can create. When you have an action represented by a cluster of assets—give it a title.

Take my example above. I combined my work as a trainer with my love of wellness and writing to discover a new writing niche. But what if I stretched my imagination and combined these assets with my interest in fashion? Maybe I could write for a company that sells fitness clothing.

Step Three: Save Your Work
When you are finished with Step Two, you'll have a bunch of actions you *could* take. Take photos of them or simply transfer them to your journal or a computer document. Hold onto this. You'll be using it in the next set of quests that help you create goals.

Game Play Tips
- Have fun with this. Remember: You're just brainstorming. You don't have to actually do any of the actions you come up with. Playing with your assets, knowledge, and passions will help you see possibilities from resources you may not have thought of connecting.
- Power up the possibilities by working with your allies (see "26. Identify Your Allies" on page 91)! Find a colleague (or several) to do this quest with you. Decide ahead of time if you want to combine assets to create new opportunities. When we combine our assets, knowledge, and passions with those of others— ka-boom! It's positively explosive and lots of fun.
- As you can see from the examples, your work might lead to finding potential writing niches and projects—and that's good, because this book is about how you can create more! But you might also find new projects in many areas of your life. Pretty cool!

For the Win
Isn't it amazing to know that all the crazy things you've done in your life might lead to bigger and better things? Now that you've seen how this works, maybe it's time to take a look in your refrigerator. What can you combine to make a delicious meal?

9. CHOOSE YOUR PROJECT

Every writer or wanna-be writer has ideas for books. The problem isn't finding an idea, it's choosing one.

— Jo Linsdell

When I meet with new clients, I ask: "What one project would you like to finish by the end of the year?"

Usually clients know the answer immediately. Then they say, "But I'd also like to write…" and present a long list of project ideas.

I'm no different. I have more ideas than I have time. When I do get time to write, it's tempting to flit back and forth between projects, like a bee searching for the best source of pollen.

Most creative people have a million good ideas floating around in their brains. We jot them in our notebooks and on our to-do lists, but juggling too many potential projects becomes a huge obstacle to finishing any of them.

This quest will help you choose a single project to focus on. Instead of juggling a dozen projects at one time, it's helpful to choose one project and schedule time to work on it. (At the most, we can create two projects at once—writing one and revising a second one or writing one and researching a second one.)

The Quest

Step One: Review
Review your vision statements from the quests "1. Vision Your Epic Wins" on page 20, "2. Capture Your Vision Daily" on page 23, and "3. Learn from Envy" on page 26. Underline anything that sounds like a project you want to work on. Go through your idea notebooks, computer, journals—anywhere you've stashed your secret thoughts—and make a great big list of ideas.

Step Two: Pick Favorites
Look at your list of possible project ideas and star the three to five ideas that you're most excited about right now. These might be a mix of writing projects and other goals.

Step Three: Evaluate

Evaluate each item based on the following tests:

The Passion Test: Are you passionate about this goal? Does the idea of working on this goal energize you? Do you wake up thinking about the goal? Is your goal an accomplishment that you believe so much in that you're willing to give up time and money to achieve it? Do you feel jealous, sad, or angry when someone you know creates a project similar to yours?

The Purpose Test: Is the goal connected to your life's purpose? You need a reason to be writing a book or producing a big project, a purpose beyond yourself. Ask yourself: why am I doing this? To teach, create joy, or entertain? Purpose works best when you know who you'll be serving. Ask: who will benefit from this project?

The Definition Test: Goals that work are clear and concise. You can see the goal and know exactly what you need to do to achieve it. Many of us write vague goals like, I want to write more. or I want to work on my blog. But when you articulate a goal as a specific quest—"I will write a book of essays on change"—you know exactly what you want to accomplish and have a better chance of achieving it.

Step Four: Make Your Choice

When you've put your potential goals through the previous tests, does any one goal pass all three tests? Finally, ask yourself: What one project do I really want to finish this year?

Choose one goal to work on in the next three months…or whatever time frame works for you.

Game Play Tips

- Choosing a single project is hard. When you make your list of top projects, you might create a calendar of projects to work on in the coming year. That way, you'll have the next project to look forward to as you're finishing this one.
- Be prepared for the inner critic to throw a big stink over choosing a single project (*You should be doing more!*) or what project you choose (*Do you really think that will sell?*). Remind the critic that you're in charge and kick it out of the room. If that doesn't work, check out one of the quests on dealing with the inner critic such as "27. Name Your Villains" on page 94, "38. Examine Your Thoughts" on page 128, or "40. Lasso of Truth" on page 132.

- It can be helpful to do this quest over several days or a week. Choose a project to work on and then sit with it for a few days. If it doesn't feel right, switch to a different project.

For the Win

When we work on the right project, we feel joyful. It's like having a new friend or love interest. We think about it all the time, are willing to skip other events to work on it, and lose track of time when we're engaged in the project. Of course, it's not always like this—what in life is? But when the project is right, we get just enough of the positive feeling to keep coming back for more.

10. WRITE GOALS THAT WORK

When you discover your mission, you will feel its demand. It will fill you with enthusiasm and a burning desire to get to work on it.

– W. Clement Stone

I work with a lot of people who approach me because they can't accomplish their goals. They want to write a book or launch a blog, but they can't seem to get around to it. Life gets in the way.

Once you've chosen your project, it's time to write your project goal. And believe me, the way you phrase your goal matters. A poorly worded goal gets stuffed in a journal and forgotten about. But a well-worded goal can be used every day to help you achieve your dreams! This quest will help you write goals that work.

The Quest

Goals that work are:

- Driven by your passion and purpose
- Defined in specific and concrete terms
- Connected to a plan

When you phrase your goals to include a plan—when, where, and how you will achieve them—you increase your chances of success. You know what steps you need to take to achieve your goal. You have a clear sense of what you need to do and when and where you will do it.

Write

Compose a goal statement using the following formula:

[When], *I will* [where and what] *so that I can achieve my goal of* [state goal].

Here are some examples of goal statements that include all of these elements:

After work each day, I will stop at the coffee shop and write for an hour so that I can achieve my goal of writing my book on public speaking.

Every Saturday and Sunday morning, I will sit at my sewing machine and make scarves so I can achieve my goal of finishing enough scarves to have a table at the school's annual craft sale.

Each night before bed, I will sit in my writing chair and write a scene so that I can achieve my goal of writing my novel.

Game Play Tips

- To make your goal more useful, at the end of your goal statement add a note about WHY you're writing a book. For example, you might write:

  After work each day, I will stop at the coffee shop and write for an hour so that I can achieve my goal of writing my book to help my clients learn how to overcome their fear of public speaking.

- When you finish writing your goal, copy it onto a big sheet of paper or large index card and post it somewhere you can see it every day! (Or go to a site like Canva and make a graphic that you can post on your computer!)
- Keep a copy of your goal statement near your desk, datebook, and in any other place that might be helpful. When you receive offers to do something else during your writing time, it will help to know that you are already booked, working hard at accomplishing a goal.

For the Win

Once we've created a goal with all of the elements—what, when, where, and why—we have clarity. We not only know where we're going but how we're going to get there. We can set up our lives to help us achieve this goal, easily dealing with the tasks and problems that threaten to get in the way.

11. PLAY WITH GOALS

The best is the enemy of the good.

– Voltaire

I often work with clients who struggle to articulate their goals. While they catch glimpses of what they might want to do, they resist choosing. They have many ideas—all exciting, many good, but none of them perfect. They worry about choosing the wrong thing. What if they spend a whole year working on something that doesn't work?

They're dealing with the tyranny of perfection. They want their writing work to be good, to sell, to influence their clients, so they try to find the perfect project. According to Professor Brené Brown, the pursuit of perfection leads to life-paralysis. She says:

> Life paralysis refers to all of the opportunities we miss because we're too afraid to put anything out in the world that could be imperfect. It's also all of the dreams that we don't follow because of our deep fear of failing, making mistakes, and disappointing others.[11]

But if we wait to create the perfect resolution, we'll never do anything. We need to craft the good-enough resolution. We need to try to move forward on a single project even if we move slowly and imperfectly!

This quest is a bit different than the others. It gives you three ways to try out new goals before you commit to them. Try one or all of them.

The Quest

If you did the last quest ("10. Write Goals that Work" on page 45), you've created a well-worded goal. Use one or more of these tools to try out your goal and modify as needed. If you haven't created your goal, this quest offers the perfect opportunity for you to play with potential goals and see what works.

The Short-Term Goal or Try Before You Buy

I recently heard about a dog shelter that allows adoptive families to try out dogs for five days before making a final commitment. That allows families the time to see if the new relationship works. Why not use the same technique for your goal? Try it out for a week or two and see how it goes. Maybe you're an afternoon writer who'd like to write in the morning. Or you're a wannabe writer who hopes to use a lunch hour at work to create a blog. Try it for a few weeks, observe what works and what doesn't work—and then evaluate the results. Once you've collected some data on how the new habit works in your life, you can make a more permanent commitment to your resolution.

The Learning Resolution or Becoming a Student

Sometime we can avoid that scary "I have to do it perfectly" feeling by switching our role from expert to student. Instead of setting resolutions that put us in the expert seat (*I'm going to become the best damn novelist in the world*), why not try a learning goal (*I am going to learn about how to create better characters*)? With this type of goal, we might take a class, read a book, or connect with a mentor. But we can also approach any resolution with an attitude of learning by getting curious, asking questions, and exploring possibilities. So the novel writer might take a class or simply ask what makes a novel great and work on applying those characteristics to her writing.

The Small-Step Resolution or The Way of the Turtle

Being a life-long turtle fan, I like the idea of taking small steps. Think about your writing goals and then imagine some small steps toward that goal. Maybe you want to write more. Why not add five minutes to your writing time each day? Perhaps you'd like to learn how to use social media. Take 30 minutes a week to observe one of the social media platforms. Whenever you come up with a small step, ask yourself: is this small enough? If you feel excited, then it probably is. If you're still afraid, make the step even smaller. Increase or shift your steps by listening to your inner turtle sense!

Game Play Tips

- You never, ever have to live with a goal forever. Tweak it, dump it, or craft a new one. You're in charge!
- This quest offers three ways to try out goals—but maybe you have your own ideas. Use your secret identity to create your own method for playing with a goal. If you're Doctor Dreamer with the superpower of daydreaming and visioning, you'll dream about your goal for a week or two, trying it on in your head before you work on it in real life. Or maybe you're the Lightening Warrior who has great success with short bursts of energy. You might play with a goal over a weekend or a short retreat.

For the Win

There are many ways to get things done. Playing with goals provides a fun opportunity to jump into the work of achieving our goals. Sometimes when we play with a goal instead of doggedly pursuing it, we can start and finish projects without experiencing the tyranny of perfection.

12. ELIMINATE CONFLICTING GOALS

For most of us, though, the problem is not a lack of goals but rather too many of them.

– Roy F. Baumeister

I had a meltdown. I'm not proud of it. It happens every summer, no matter how much I plan. School ends, summer begins, and my routine goes to the dogs. This past year, I vowed it would be different. Yes, the kids would be home. Yes, I had more work than usual. But I had a plan that would make it possible for me to write, exercise, work, and spend time with my spouse and children.

By the end of the first day I was in tears, searching online for summer boarding schools. In the moments between dogs and children puking, the basement flooding, and my email program crashing, I accomplished no work. Words written: zero. Pages edited: zero. Miles walked: well, quite a few, if you count running up and down stairs with buckets and sponges.

In retrospect, this experience gave me something more valuable than writing time: a lesson in conflicting goals. When we set multiple goals that conflict with each other, we don't make much progress on any of them. So my goals to write, exercise, edit, and take care of kids all in the same, precious chunk of time was a set up for failure. I couldn't write or edit with the distraction of my kids coming in every few minutes. I also couldn't attend to my kids while I was trying to write and edit. The result of trying to achieve multiple goals at once? Frustration.

We live in a goal-driven society. We talk about goals at work and at home, at school and in our sports activities. We have goals for our selves, our families, and our pets. We even set goals for our vacations. With this flurry of goal setting activity, you'd think we'd be brilliant at getting things done. But what most of us excel at is being busy. We have too many goals and distractions competing for our attention.

What's the solution? In this quest, we'll put on our scientist hat and gather the data from our life. Once we know what's getting in the way of achieving our goals, we can adjust our expectations, revise our goals, and get back to work.

The Quest

Use your journal to reflect on the following questions. You might use the data you collected in previous quests to provide additional information for this quest.

What's your primary goal? You know, the project you want or need to get done no matter what.

What goals might conflict with this goal? In the movies, creative people face serious, sometimes life-threatening conflicts when they work: drinking, drugs, ghosts, or kidnapping. In real life, the things that interrupt our primary goals are usually good stuff. It's not a choice between creating and watching reality television all day. It's usually a choice between creating and taking care of a sick friend or creating and earning an income. Keep that in mind as you review your life. Look at:

- *Other goals.* Does your primary goal compete with other goals in your life? For example, the goals of expanding a business and writing a novel conflict with each other because both take an extraordinary amount of time and energy. Sometimes writers sabotage their success by having too many writing projects going at once. What goal(s) do you need to drop to accomplish your primary goal?
- *Time.* Does your primary goal compete with your other time commitments? My goals of writing and exercising first thing in the morning conflict with each other because they occupy the same time slot. When can you create time to work on your primary goal? Schedule the time.
- *Distractions.* What external distractions consistently interrupt you when you're working on your primary goal? How can you create the space you need to work on your goal?

How can you accomplish your primary goal? Once you've analyzed your goals, reaffirm the primary goal you've chosen to work on. It's fine if you come to the conclusion that you were drunk or crazy or both when you set the goal of writing a novel while you were also finishing your doctoral dissertation or starting a business. Choose the goal that's most pressing right now. Even though you'd rather write a novel, you may need to set it aside for a time while you finish your dissertation.

Schedule dedicated time each day or week to work on your primary goal. Then make this time sacred: no distractions.

Let go of the goals, commitments, and other distractions that interfere with achieving your primary goal.

Game Play Tips

- Letting go of conflicting goals is hard. It will mean disappointing people and missing out on some events. Know that going into the quest. And know you don't have to explain to anyone why you aren't volunteering to be neighborhood watch captain this year.
- This quest has two parts: identifying what doesn't work and then letting go of it. Saying no can be hard, especially when we have to say no to things we love. The next quest will help you do just that.
- If you come to the conclusion that this is not the time for you to take on a big writing project, you might work on a small creative project each day. If working for twenty minutes a day conflicts with your other goals, then try writing for fifteen or even five minutes a day. Don't forget the small step method (see "29. Take Small Steps" on page 100)! Five minutes a day can yield big results.

For the Win

Many wise people have said that in order to solve a problem, we must first recognize we have one. This quest helped you do just that—discover what was getting in the way of working on your central goal. It's a quest you can return to whenever you feel too busy and are frustrated by not making progress on your key vision.

13. DEVELOP A LIFE PRIORITY LIST

Never say 'no' to adventures. Always say 'yes,' otherwise you'll lead a very dull life.

– Ian Fleming

Most of us know what we're never up for. Here's part of my list: roller coasters, cats (I'm sadly allergic), and proofreading. Though I've been known to take on a proofreading project when I'm desperate for extra money, it usually leads to overeating chocolate and binge watching *Veronica Mars*.

But despite having a clear idea of what we don't want to do, many of us don't make time for the activities we're passionate about—like writing. We do what we have to do to make a living, and then take care of the tasks necessary to make a life. With the energy we have left over, we fulfill our wants. But often we're too tired to remember to connect to the activities that bring us joy or lead us closer to living our vision of the ideal life.

In my book *Write-A-Thon*, I talk about how using a life priority list can help us say yes to what matters. A life priority list or "absolute yes" list are the five activities that we are so passionate about we will always say yes to them. The tool comes from coach Cheryl Richardson's book *Take Time for Your Life*.[12] This kind of list makes responding to invites much easier—if it doesn't fit the list, it gets an immediate, "no." Here's an excerpt:

For years, I have made use of a life priority list—a list that names the five people and activities I will always make a priority. My list is: Self, Writing, Family, Friends, and my Coaching business. Any invitation that fits within this list frequently gets a yes. Any activity not on the list needs to prove its worth before I can say yes.[13]

In this quest, you'll create your own life priority list.

The Quest

If you've worked through this book in order, you've done several quests that have helped you vision your future and write goals. If you haven't done those quests and you have difficulty with this quest, you may want to do those quests first.

What Do You Value?

Ask yourself: *What people, events, work, and recreational activities are most important to me?* Make a list.

Choose Five

If you end up with a list of ten or fifteen items, then it's time to choose five. And yes—although some people suggest you could have up to ten things on your list, don't! Respect your own boundaries and limit yourself to five. Here's how:

Review. Look at your "Vision Your Epic Wins" vision statements and goal statements. What items come up repeatedly?

Combine. Are any of the items on your list activities or interests that could be combined? Maybe you have plays, concerts, and movies on your list. This could be combined under Arts Events.

Challenge. If you really want to write or make art and you have more than five items on your list, ask:
- Would I say yes to this instead of writing or making art? If not, dump it!
- Would I say yes to this if I had to do it for free? If not, take it off the list!
- Would I say yes to this if I wasn't worried about pleasing others? If not, cut it.
- Would I say yes to this if I had to pay to do it? We pay for what we love doing, but often forget that when we give up our time, we're paying in a different way.
- Would I say yes to this if I had a year to live?
- Do I need this to be an "absolute yes" or could I make it a "maybe?" Remove the maybes!

Explore

Whew! You did it! Now that you have just five items, add a few sentences to describe what each item means for you. It's helpful to be specific here. For example, while family is definitely on my list, and part of that includes helping out at my children's schools, I am clear that I want to help in ways that allow me to use my strengths. That means I usually teach a writing class or two a year but never volunteer to take on administrative tasks, like being class parent.

Practice

The absolute yes list means nothing until you act on it. Take that absolute yes list on the road. And by on the road, I mean take it to your calendar, your desktop, and anywhere else you do work. Next time someone invites you to do something, check the list. And don't say yes unless the activity fits with one of your priorities and does not conflict with your primary goal—see "12. Eliminate Conflicting Goals" on page 49.

Game Play Tips

- Challenge the yeses, especially if you are a people pleaser.
- If you use the absolute yes list and still say yes even when you want to say no, use the challenge questions when you have a decision to make.
- Consider how your Secret Identity can help you say no to the tasks and events that are not on your life priority list. While you might have trouble saying no, maybe The Magnificent Magnetic Master loves to dismiss anything that doesn't have the magnetic power to woo!
- Change it up! If you use the list for a few weeks or months and it doesn't feel like it's working, it might not be. Major life events or simply changes in seasons can shift the items on our list. Review the quest again and revise your list.

For the Win

The absolute yes list works because it takes the angst out of making decisions. We've pre-decided what's important to us so that when someone asks us to do something, we can consult our list. Of course, many of us will agonize anyway—it's a bad habit that we need to learn to break. And the list will help us do that.

14. LEARN TO SAY NO

*[Innovation] comes from saying no to 1,000 things to make sure we
don't get on the wrong track or try to do too much.*

– Steve Jobs

I should have said no. I had agreed to a 7:00 AM committee meeting. I
love the early morning hours and dedicate it to thought, writing, and
exercise. For the most part, I do not see clients, attend meetings, or even
check email until 10:00 AM. But somehow, my inner guardian had been
sleeping when a friend asked if I could "help with the PTA." Suddenly, I
was on the board and attending a 7:00 AM meeting. Thankfully, my inner
guardian woke up. I resigned from the board and agreed to work on a
project with the school that fit with both my strengths and availability.

"I should have said no." How often do you repeat those words to yourself? I'm not just talking about volunteering. How often have you:

- taken on a project that you don't have time for
- agreed to an assignment or job that doesn't interest you
- worked with a client who you already know is difficult
- taught a class for free
- taken on a project for less than fair market value

We all say yes to projects that don't work for us. Our reasons are often
good ones. We need the money, want the impressive byline, or hope to
help a good cause. But sometimes, dear ones, we say yes because we are
in the habit of saying yes. We say yes before we even think about how the
new project or responsibility will impact our lives. And here's the rub: we
sometimes need to say no to important, valuable projects and experiences
in order to say yes to the work that matters most to us. Yeah, that means
that sometimes we say no to a project that pays so that we have time to
write a nonfiction book, develop a home study course, or create a new
sculpture.

This quest will help you figure out when to say no and learn how to do it.

The Quest

If you've been working through this book in order, you've chosen your
current project goal (see "9. Choose Your Project" on page 42), reviewed
potential conflicting goals (see "12. Eliminate Conflicting Goals" on page
49), and created a life priority list (see "13. Develop a Life Priority List"
on page 52). You have all that you need to improve your ability to say no.

If you haven't done those things, you may want to go back and do
them before completing this quest.

Practice

For the following month, when you get invited to do anything, say, "Let me think about that and get back to you." I don't care who is calling you—the head of a publishing house or the President of the United States—do not say yes or no right away. Take time to weigh the invitation against your primary goal, life priority list, and life's current demands. Ask yourself how this new experience fits with what you are working towards. If it fits, say yes. If not, exercise the right to say, "No." Then get back to your core project or creative work!

Reflect

After doing this for a month, review your progress:

- When were you tempted to say yes?
- When did you say yes when you wished you'd said no?
- What could you do differently?

Game Play Tips

- My therapist used to say to me, "Too much of a good thing is still too much." As you sort through opportunities, know that you'll have to say no to good things as well as less desirable activities.
- You'll be most tempted to say yes to new projects at the beginning of a new month, a new season, or a new year, because the days feel open and full of possibility. Take a breath and wait before you say yes.
- It can also be tempting to say yes to invitations when you've finished a big project and are relishing that feeling of emptiness. Take another deep breath and a weekend to think it over before you give your answer.
- You might be excited and eager to take on activities that appeal to you and fit your absolute yes list. Before saying yes, ask yourself if these activities fit your life right now. Do they conflict with your main creative goal? Could they be done at a different time?

For the Win

When I try to do too much and say yes to obligations that don't make my heart sing, I end up letting go of writing time. And then I feel resentful. I'm learning to say no instead. Here's what Anne Lamott says about saying no:

> My therapist, Rita, has convinced me that every time I say yes when I mean no, I am abandoning myself, and I end up feeling used or resentful or frantic. But when I say no when I mean no, it's so sane and healthy that it creates a little glade around me in which I can get the nourishment I need. Then I help and serve people from a place of real abundance and health.[14]

When you say no when you mean no, you leave time in your life to say yes to what matters to you. And that's always a good thing.

15. LET IT GO

But when we really delve into the reasons for why we can't let something go, there are only two: an attachment to the past or a fear for the future.

– Marie Kondo

In Marie Kondo's popular book, *The Life-Changing Magic of Tidying Up*, she invites readers to sort through their possessions by type. For example, the person who has an overstuffed closet would dump all of her clothes in the center of the room. Then she would pick up each item and ask a single question, "Does this spark joy?" If so, she would keep it. If not, toss it—but not before thanking the item for its service.

This quest will help you let go of the tasks and projects that don't fit with your current purpose or goals.

The Quest

This process is designed to support you in letting go of the projects, commitments, and tasks that don't work for you—leaving you with the goals you are committed to achieving right now. You've probably already chosen a single project to work on, but if you haven't, this process can also be used to decide what project to focus on.

In this quest, you'll be thinking about everything you do—from home chores to work tasks. As you go through this process, include any parts of your life that feel overwhelming.

Phase One: Create Your Big List of Tasks

STEP ONE: LIST IT

On a large sheet of paper, jot down everything you do by category: creative or core projects, work tasks, home commitments, networking events, and any other activity that claims your time.

As you record your projects and tasks, pay attention to how you feel. Does the idea of the task spark energy or leave you feeling drained? Note your energy levels in this way:

- Use the plus symbol (+) to indicate tasks that energize you.
- Use a minus symbol (-) to note tasks that drain you.

STEP TWO: QUESTION IT

Once you've finished making the list, review each item and ask this question: "Does this activity spark joy?" Ask this even if you've already marked it with a "+" or a "-."

If the answer is still yes, circle the item.

If the answer is no, then ask a few more questions and circle the ones that get a yes:

- Does this project or task bring other rewards? (Like a paycheck!)
- Does this project or task serve a purpose?
- Will this project lead to long-term benefits?

Here's an example. I exercise every morning at the gym. At 6 AM, the idea of leaving the house to work out does not spark joy. But the practice of exercising brings other rewards and serves a larger purpose. I get the immediate reward of socializing with my workout buddies. And the practice also fulfills a larger purpose: I stay fit.

STEP THREE: REVIEW WHAT'S LEFT

Take a look at what's not circled and consider:

- Can you let go of these tasks forever? Cross them out.
- Can you let go of these tasks for now? Transfer them to a "maybe someday" list of projects, commitments, and tasks.
- Can you delegate these tasks? Note your plan for delegating the tasks. For example, if your task is "Clean the house," then the plan to delegate might be: hire a cleaning service.

STEP FOUR: CHECK YOUR WORK

Finally, take a look at all the circled items and ask: Is there anything else I can let go of for now? Cross out these items, find another solution, or put them on your maybe someday list.

Pay special attention to any circled item that has a minus sign next to it. Sometimes we circle tasks that drain our energy because they serve a larger purpose. For example, sending out invoices after a writing project might drain us, but it serves an important purpose—it helps us get paid! If you can't drop a task that drains you, consider:

- Can you make the task easier by creating a template?
- Can you make a task more fun by doing it with a colleague?
- Can you hire someone else to do it?
- Can you exchange the task with someone else?

Phase Two: Review the Yeses

If you're like me—bubbling over with ideas—you will no doubt finish phase one with more yeses than you can handle at one time. For those of us who suffer from the planning fallacy—we underestimate how long it will take to finish a task—it's important to narrow down our choices even more.

Primary Project. If you've already chosen a primary project, this should be easy. If not, it will help you do that final cut. Take a look at the yeses in the creative or core project category and ask: What one creative project will I focus on in the next three months? Everything else can go on your list of things to tackle at a different time.

Other Tasks. Review the circled items in other categories and ask:

- Will any of these get in the way of me finishing my primary project? Cross it out or create a plan to deal with it. See the suggestions under Check Your Work (above) and Game Play Tips (below) for more information on how to cope with essential tasks that interrupt our creative work, like children and pets.
- Can any of these wait until I finish my primary project? Cross it out or place it on your list of future projects.

Game Play Tips

- This quest is similar to "13. Develop a Life Priority List" on page 52. Feel free to consult your list as you do the quest or go back to the list and change it once you've completed this task.
- If letting go of an activity or work task feels especially hard, examine why you're holding onto it. Are you afraid that if you let it go, you will offend someone? Or do you worry about turning away low-paying work just in case more work won't come?
- If letting go isn't an option—perhaps you care for an elderly parent, a sick dog, or children—consider what steps you can take to lighten your burden. This may mean saying no to other things on your list, sharing the responsibility with another family member, or getting outside help.

For the Win

Watch what happens to your mood when you let go of extra projects and tasks and focus on what brings you joy. No doubt you'll finish more of your projects, but you also will have a feeling of lightness.

16. EXAMINE THE PAST

Truth walks toward us on the paths of our questions...as soon as you think you have the answer, you have closed the path and may miss vital new information. Wait awhile in the stillness, and do not rush to conclusions, no matter how uncomfortable the unknowing.

— Jacqueline Winspear

I'm a huge fan of Jacqueline Winspear's mystery series featuring Maisie Dobbs, a private investigator working just after the end of World War I. At the end of every case, detective Maisie Dobbs sits with her case map and does a reckoning. She reviews her notes, makes decisions about how to deal with any loose ends, and thinks about how she'll use what she's learned in her life and with future cases.

I think of this as balcony space—a place where we can get a bird's-eye view of our habits and practices and understand the whole of our lives. Leadership consultants Gil Rendle and Alice Mann define it this way in their book, *Holy Conversations*:

> Balcony space describes taking a position sufficiently distant from day-to-day operations and worry in order to see the larger picture. The opposite of balcony space is reactive space, in which the leader must constantly deal with the immediate person or problem that confronts him or her.[15]

At the end of a year or when we finish a big project, it can be helpful to look at what we've accomplished and do our own reckoning of sorts. This quest will help you complete your own reckoning.

The Quest
Plan at least an afternoon away from your regular work and home responsibilities. If possible, take a weekend. Make arrangements that enable you to be away from your phone, email, and social media for the duration of your balcony time.

Choose a place where you are away from your day-to-day life (and won't be interrupted)—a coffee shop, library, park, restaurant, art museum, hotel, or spa. If you have time for a longer retreat, a drive or train ride can help you to see your life from a balcony perspective.

Step One: Planning

Decide what you want to examine during your balcony time. Perhaps you want to review a period of time or a project. Many people like doing this quest at the end of a year, but it can be also helpful to do it quarterly or twice a year. Others use it as a springboard for deciding what project to work on next or how to make their business more successful. Maybe you want to evaluate what's working and what's holding you back. Set your purpose for your time away.

Gather tools to help you review and record the current picture of your life and envision a new one. You might consider taking your calendar (online or paper), a record of your income for the period you are reviewing, a journal or empty notebook, a variety of pens and markers, and inspirational books and music.

Step Two: Evaluate and Reflect

The following questions will help you get a big picture view of your life and evaluate it in relation to your goals. Adapt this to your specific goal for your balcony time.

Map your life. Using your calendar and journal, create a visual map of your days. This might be a blank calendar with times and tasks filled in or a visual rendering of a day, using colored pencils to indicate different tasks. How are you spending your time? What tasks do you do regularly? Where do you do these tasks? Include everything you can think of.

Review goals. Write down or review all of the goals you set for this year (or this quarter) and the plans that you made to accomplish them. These questions might help:

- What were your New Year's goals for your primary purpose— your writing career, art making, or other creative project?
- What projects did you hope to finish by the end of the year?
- How much money did you expect to make from your core purpose this year?
- What other tasks related to your primary purpose did you plan to take on (e.g., workshops, reading, research, mentoring, and so forth)?
- What sort of a plan did you set up to help you meet your goal?

Review life. Compare your goals with your daily schedule and projects. Use these questions to reflect:

- How have you been spending your time?
- Do your daily actions match up with your goals?
- What work have you produced so far this year?
- If you planned to make money from working on your primary purpose, are you making satisfactory progress on meeting your income and project goals?
- If not, what other projects have emerged as priorities for your work?
- Are there any energy drains or unexpected commitments that have taken up your time?

Reevaluate. If your actions match the goals you set—congrats! If not, you will need to reevaluate your goals and how you spend your time so that you can get back on track. Ask yourself:

- What am I doing that's working?
- What am I doing that's not working?
- Do I need to change my goals in any way?
- What do I need to do differently in order to meet my goals?
- How will I put this plan into action?
- How will I know if I'm achieving my goals?

Finally, consider this:

- What kinds of creative work do I want to do less of?
- What kinds of creative work do I want to do more of?

Step Three: Choose Practices

To benefit from balcony space, we need to let go of our old habits and invest in new practices. That can be tough. Most of us are pretty attached to our daily routine, and it often takes courage and a big kick in the pants to change. Now that you've been to the balcony, you know what you need to do. So do it!

If you have trouble implementing the new practices, take a look at your environment. You might need to change something to make it easier for you to create a new habit. For example, after my last trip to the balcony, I decided to revise the children's novel I wrote during a previous National Novel Writing Month. To make that happen, I ended each day by leaving the novel file open on my computer. When I woke up my computer the next day, it was the first thing I saw. I couldn't avoid working on it.

Game Play Tips

- You will have some immediate answers to these questions. Write them down and honor them. But you may also want to sit with the questions for a bit until the right answer shows up.
- If possible, make a note of your energy and passion around what you accomplished. Perhaps you achieved a big goal, like ghostwriting a book for a client or painting a large public mural, but you hated every minute of it. That's important information. Note that.
- At the end of the year, this quest can be a great tool to help us review the past year and move forward. But it also can be a helpful tool anytime you want to review, revise, and reboot.

For the Win

Examining the past allows us to be wise when we reflect on our life and work. We can be pretty hard on ourselves about what we do or do not accomplish. This tool helps us to treat it as information we can use to make helpful shifts in our practices.

17. MAKE PEACE WITH YOUR PAST

You can't undo what you've already done, but you can face up to it.
— Frank Coleridge, *Silent Hill: Downpour*

Do you ever wish you could travel back in time, and give your younger self a gentle nudge or a kick in the pants?

After her mother died suddenly, Ellyn Spragin longed to know how her mother had felt during significant moments or how she handled difficult situations. Spragin sought answers from women she admired, like Maya Angelou. She collected these letters in the book, *What I Know Now: Letters to My Younger Self*.[16] Here's what a few of the women had to say:

"Don't let anybody raise you. You've been raised."
— Maya Angelou

"Please yourself first…everything else follows."
— Macy Gray

"Try more things. Cross more lines."
— Breena Clarke

What do you wish you'd known a year ago? If your younger self possessed the wisdom you've gained over the past year, what would you have done differently? In this quest, you'll review the past, communicate with your younger self, and let go of your regrets.

The Quest

Set aside at least an hour to do this quest. If you did the quest "16. Examine the Past" on page 61, you've already reviewed your past and recorded what you did and didn't do. Use that information to help you work on this quest.

Step One: Review

Review the year past (or any amount of time that works for you). Record your successes and missteps. Did you accomplish something that surprised you? Did one of your successes bring you more joy than you expected it to? Is there anything you regret? Something you wish you'd done (or done sooner)? What did you spend too much time worrying about or crying over?

Step Two: Write
Once you've completed your list, write your younger self a letter. What advice or encouragement would you give to yourself?

Step Three: Forgive
Let yourself off the hook for past mistakes or missteps.

- Start by offering yourself compassion: *Dear one, I understand. You did the best you could with _____.*
- Then forgive yourself: *I forgive you for ____.*
- Let go: *I let go of hoping to have a different past. I promise not to beat up on myself for past mistakes or missteps.*
- Repeat as needed.

Step Four: Celebrate
As a coach, I'm constantly reminding my clients about the successes they downplay or ignore. I encourage my clients to celebrate each and every win. And I want you to do the same thing. Sometime this week, find a way to celebrate what went well this year. And remember, no accomplishment is too small to celebrate!

Game Play Tips
- It can be helpful to do this quest in two sessions. In the first session, reflect on the past. In the second session, write yourself a letter and offer forgiveness for the past.
- When you write your compassionate letter, it may be helpful to use the kind things that your allies (see "26. Identify Your Allies" on page 91) have said to you in the past.
- Consider creating a ritual to offer forgiveness to yourself and move forward. It can be as simple as burning the regrets and toasting to your fresh start.

For the Win
When asked about the secret to his longevity, the 92-year-old producer Norman Lear said, "There are two small words that are important and mostly overlooked: *over* and *next*. When something is over, it is over. Everything is about what comes next."[17] Now that you've reflected on the past year, it's time to stop dwelling on anything you've done or failed to do last year, this year, or any other year: it's over. Now focus on what you want to do NEXT!

PART TWO: DISCOVER AND IMPLEMENT YOUR BEST PRACTICES

18. Examine Traits of Success
Examine and collect the traits of successful authors and artists.

19. Detect Your Genius Time
Discover the time of day when you do best on intellectual and creative tasks.

20. Find Your Where
Seek the ideal location for your creative work.

21. Discern Your Best Practices
Review your most productive creative sessions and identify the skills, practices, and external elements present.

22. Recognize Your Strengths
Examine best practices to discover your strongest traits, skills, and projects.

23. Find Wisdom in Weaknesses
Review your least productive creative sessions to understand the situation, see the strengths that emerge, and learn how to create successful situations.

24. Uncover Secret Super Powers
Investigate eccentricities to discover secret strengths.

25. Discover Favorite Power-ups
Examine life to find the practices that increase or renew your energy.

26. Identify your Allies
Discover and connect with supportive colleagues.

27. Name your Villains
Find real and imaginary critics and create a plan to defeat them.

28. Develop a Writing Habit
Learn the habit loop and create your own.

29. Take Small Steps
Break a big goal into small, manageable chunks.

30. Know the What
Learn prewriting exercises to eliminate the fear of the blank page.

31. Cluster Tasks
Group together similar tasks and schedule them in the calendar.

32. Automate Decisions
Discover decisions that can be made ahead of time.

33. Utilize Templates
Create key templates to ease your workload.

34. Organize Your Office
Clean out and organize writing space.

35. Journal to Boost Productivity
Examine multiple ways journaling can support your creative life.

36. Move Your Body
Consider multiple ways to stay active throughout the day.

37. Read as a Writer
Develop a reading plan and follow it.

18. EXAMINE TRAITS OF SUCCESS

The whole problem with the world is that fools and fanatics are always so certain of themselves, and wiser people so full of doubts.

– Bertrand Russell

I follow many writers and creatives on Twitter, Instagram, and Facebook. When they share their habits, successes, and even their failures, I feel encouraged to write more. And guess what? Imagining what successful creatives do—how they schedule time to create, overcome obstacles, and move forward in the face of rejection—can help us do the same.

According to the research, when we consider the positive traits of a group, rather than an individual, and then compare ourselves to the group, we become twice as likely to act like they do. Jane McGonigal wrote about the study in her book, *SuperBetter: A Revolutionary Approach to Getting Stronger, Happier, Braver, and More Resilient*. In the study, researchers separated participants into two groups.[18] One was asked to record the traits of Superman and the other was invited to list the traits of superheroes in general. Afterwards, the participants were asked to sign up to tutor youth. When researchers looked at who signed up to volunteer, the participants who thought about superheroes in general were twice as likely to volunteer than those who reflected on Superman. When researchers followed up with the study's participants three months later, they found that these people were "*four times* as likely to actually show up for a volunteering session."[19]

When we consider the positive traits of a group, we compare ourselves to the group—looking primarily for similarities. This practice makes us more likely to act like they do. *But there's a caveat:* This seems to work only when participants thought about the traits of an entire group of heroes versus a single one. When they reflected on the traits of a single exemplary superhero, they tended to notice only the differences and "judged themselves to be less helpful."[20] As a result, the participants were less likely to reach out and help others.

This bit of scientific research provides the inspiration for this quest: discovering the traits of successful people.

The Quest

Describe the characteristics of the group you most want to be like: such as, successful writers, entrepreneurs, artists, or speakers. Think of these successful people as a group—not one specific person—and make a list of their behaviors, characteristics, values, practices, and lifestyle. Record your answers in your journal.

If you're stuck, access your memory of artist talks, interviews, and conversations. If you don't have much information, read up on the habits of successful people. Read articles and books about the habits shared by successful people. Or imagine what productive people do and write about that. If it helps, borrow what you know about successful, productive people in other fields and use those traits for your list. Take 5-10 minutes to describe things like:

- What does the day of a successful author, entrepreneur, speaker, or artist look like?
- What are their habits?
- What does their creative schedule look like?
- What do they do besides create?
- How do they overcome obstacles or writer's block?
- How do they react to setbacks?
- How do they deal with rejection?

Game Play Tips

- When you're finished, use the list of information to create a document such as:
  › Best Practices of Successful Writers
  › The Habits of Successful Artists
  › The Mindset of High-Earning Creatives
- Art it up! Take your descriptions and create a collage that reflects 5-10 of the characteristics of successful, productive people in your field.
- As you reflect on the practices of successful people, consider how you can act as if you are part of the group. Are there practices you will adopt? Is there a uniform you can wear? A mantra you can say? Embrace these signs of success as well as your place in the group. You belong with the winners!

For the Win

By the end of this quest, you'll have a much better idea of what successful creatives do. And hopefully, you will be claiming your own success. That's your challenge, gamers.

19. DETECT YOUR GENIUS TIME

I have nothing to declare except my genius.

— Oscar Wilde

According to scientific research, our bodies peak for physical, social, and intellectual tasks at specific times of day.[21] Researchers offer broad suggestions about when we do best at various activities. For example, many of us do well at intellectual tasks during the late morning while we excel at creativity in the evening when we are tired and more open to new ideas. But even scientists admit that peak working times are different for each of us. Though some people can be classified as early birds or night owls, many people don't fit easily into any category.

This is where genius time comes in. Genius time is that part of the day when you are best able to work on your primary purpose. This quest will help you discover your genius time and the practices that support you in your creative process. My primary purpose is writing—and my genius time is mornings. That doesn't mean I cannot write at other times of day; it just means that I don't write as easily in those hours. I don't want to waste my mornings with email, social media, or meetings. I need to use those precious hours to write. But your primary purpose might be making art or coding computer games. When you examine your life, you might discover that your genius time is in the afternoon or just before bed or over the lunch hour. Your job is to protect and nurture your genius time no matter what happens. This multi-step quest will help you do just that.

The Quest

Use your journal, datebook, an online app, or a combination of the three to complete this quest.

Step One: Map Your Energy

Take a look at your most productive days. Map when you've performed like a genius at social, intellectual, creative, and physical tasks. Pro Tip: Your genius time for each type of activity will probably be at different times of day. I'm a writing mastermind at 7:00 AM but don't make me talk to anyone. (*Mornings: Social Dolt, Writing Genius; Early Afternoons: Social Wannabe, Writing Dolt*). You might also have genius times that overlap—perhaps you're good at both social and intellectual tasks in the mornings. This is okay. Just get it all down on paper, real or virtual.

If you find it difficult to recollect your best times for working on writing and other creative projects, that's okay. During the next week or two, keep track of your tasks and performance. Throughout the day, list what you do. At the end of the day, review the list and note the type of task you were doing throughout the day (if it's not immediately evident). Examples include writing, creating, thinking, social media, social engagement, physical activity, watching television, and so forth. After you have a complete list of what you accomplished, then record your energy level for each task. You can note your energy level with a simple + for engaged energy and a – for negative energy. Or, you can use terms like H (high), L (low), and M (medium).

Spend a week or two experimenting with working on your primary purpose at different parts of the day and recording your experience. Then review the results. When did you tend to be most productive as a writer? When did you tend to be most productive at other tasks? Can you build your time around these energy shifts?

Step Two: Choose and Schedule Your Project

What's the one project you want to make progress on this week during your genius time? Maybe you want to work on your book, blog, or stories? Or perhaps you have a major business presentation coming up and you need to use your time to prepare for that. Choose one project to work on during your genius time.

Before you launch headfirst into the week, working like crazy on all of the tasks you need to accomplish, create a schedule. If possible, match your one project to your intellectual and creative genius time. When I say schedule, I mean more than "think about it"—as in, *I think I might write tomorrow after work.* Note the following information in your calendar or journal:

- *When* will I work on this project?
- *Where* will I work? Is the setting conducive to what I need to do? Do I have what I need to get work done?
- *What* will I work on? You know the big project you want to work on, now choose the chunk that you will work on each day—or at least for the first day in your schedule.
- *How* will I handle interruptions or distractions? What might interrupt your plan? How will you deal with that? How will you stick to your genius time when the kids are screaming or friends invite you out for drinks or a client needs you or you're weary and just want to take a nap? Decide now.

Step Three: Honor the Genius Time

Put your butt in your chair and work on your project. If something happens and you miss a day, forgive yourself. And show up again the next day.

Game Play Tips

- Solidify your plan to use your genius time for your creative work by repeating a mantra like: *When I get home from work, I will write for 20 minutes on my nonfiction book.*
- Record your mantra on paper and post it where you can see it. (Cheesy—yes. But it works!)
- Set up your workspace ahead of time—like you might set the table for dinner—so that when it's genius time, you'll be ready to create.
- Throughout the day or the day before, imagine yourself in your space, successfully creating.
- It can help to schedule your other tasks according to your energy flow. Once you get used to this, you'll never go back!

For the Win

It has taken me a really long time to honor my genius time and NOT feel guilty. You may need to accept that you're going to feel like a fraud when you tell people you cannot meet for a networking event because you are writing or creating. If it helps, don't tell them what you'll be doing (and definitely don't confess that you can't take a meeting because you've got "genius time"). Just say: I can't meet. I'm in another meeting. And you are: with your muse.

20. FIND YOUR WHERE

Instead of thinking outside the box, get rid of the box.

– Deepak Chopra

Where do you work best—home or away?

Some creatives work well in a home office or studio. *T Magazine*, a publication of the New York Times, regularly presents photo-essays featuring the offices of famous writers. Julian Barnes writes in his home study in North London, using an old IBM typewriter on a U-shaped desk. Jhumpa Lahiri works on a small desk in the dining room of her apartment in Rome, overlooking the Alban Hills.[22] A friend of mine has dedicated a room of her basement to making art, installing new windows and a special sink for washing up.

Other creatives need to escape their homes to focus on work, finding office space in a pub, coffee shop, or hotel. Mystery novelist Brad Parks writes at Hardees. L. Frank Baum wrote many of the Oz books at the Hotel del Coranado between 1904 and 1910. Maya Angelou rented a hotel room as well, where she'd go early every morning to write. (She also liked to sip a glass of sherry while she wrote.)

When it comes to discovering the perfect place to write or create—or finding your *where*—there are no hard and fast rules. Some people want a room with a view, finding the vista inspiring. Others get distracted by what's happening outside their window, whether it's a squirrel scaling the bird feeder or a fight breaking out across the street. Ultimately, you need to discover what type of space helps you work best. In this quest, you'll try working in various places to discover the one that works for you.

The Quest

For the next week, you'll seek out your *where* by writing in various spaces both at home and away.

Home

Set aside a dedicated space to work on your creative project. It can be a home office, a desk in a corner, the end of your dining room table, or a favorite chair. Try to avoid places that you associate with other tasks—like your bed (sleeping!), the television room (movies!), or the kitchen counter (food!). Gather your supplies and set up a makeshift home office or studio. If you share your space with others, keep your supplies in a box or bag and stash them in a safe spot between writing sessions.

Away

Work in a public space like a library, coffee shop, restaurant, bar, or other venue. For people who work away from home, a backpack or tote bag packed with your most important supplies can help ease the transition into work.

Reflect

- After each creative session, reflect on how it went.
- What worked about each venue?
- What didn't work?
- Were there certain tasks that went better at home and others that worked better away?

Choose

Once you've worked in multiple environments, choose what works best for you. Create a note in your journal about your ideal *where*:

> *In my ideal* where, *I would write each morning in my home office. I would be free to shut the door and work without the children or my spouse interrupting me. After lunch, I would take my writing to the library or coffee shop, where I would review my work, revise, and imagine the next day's writing work.*

Game Play Tips

- When you're working at home, try out different rooms or areas. If the dining room table doesn't work, how about the porch? If you tend to fall asleep when you are sitting, try a standing desk.
- Try different locations outside of the house—and play around with whether you work better with the quiet of a library or the white noise of a coffee shop.
- Recognize that you might be more productive in different places depending on what project you're working on. Some writers prefer to draft their books in the quiet of their home office, but then like to revise their work in a coffee shop or bar.

For the Win

When we find our ideal working spot and use it repeatedly, we're one step closer to making our creative work a habit. Think about how this works with brushing your teeth. You've no doubt chosen a bathroom to brush your teeth in. You'd probably never brush your teeth in the kitchen sink or in your bedroom, unless that's where the best sink is. It will be the same with your creative work. Once you have a place, you will treat it as the place you go to create. And soon it will become your habit.

21. DISCERN YOUR BEST PRACTICES

One hasn't become a writer until one has distilled writing into a habit, and that habit has been forced into an obsession. Writing has to be an obsession. It has to be something as organic, physiological and psychological as speaking or sleeping or eating.

– Niyi Osundare

After coaching and teaching people about writing books for many years, I've noticed that every person has unique practices to support their work.

One writer I met made it a daily practice to copy a work of poetry or the chapter of a favorite book into her journal before each writing session. This practice eased her into writing and inspired her creativity. Aaron Sorkin, the creator of *The West Wing* and *The Social Network*, paces and acts out his own dialogue. One of my colleagues writes the first draft of her novels by hand in a notebook. She uses the same composition book for character sketches and plot notes.

Each of us has habits that support our productivity. Our best practices may come from our education, our day job, or our work as a writer. And we may not even be aware of what we do. No more! In this quest, you'll detect your best practices.

The Quest

You will need your journal for this quest.

Step One: Collect the Data

Select three of your most productive work sessions. If you have difficulty remembering these, review your calendar for examples. Or take a look at some of your finished projects—what were your most productive sessions leading up to completing those projects? You can also look at your writing sessions for school or work, work sessions for other creative projects, or journaling.

In your journal, list each session. Write only on the left side of the page, leaving a blank column on the right side of the page. Leave enough room for each entry so that you can write a short description of what happened and answer the following questions:

- What project were you working on?
- Was the writing project for someone else or yourself?
- How close were you to the deadline?
- When were you working?
- Where were you working?

- What was going on externally? (What was happening around you?)
- What was happening internally? (What were you feeling physically and emotionally?)
- What did you accomplish?
- What habits, practices, and tools helped you do your work?
- What did you have difficulty accomplishing and what did you do that helped you overcome the challenge?
- What distracted you and how did you overcome distractions to move forward?

Step Two: Decode the Data

You now have tons of information about what works for you. You may even have an intuitive sense of what your ideal working situation looks like. Now it's time to see what the data has to say.

Review the records of your most productive work sessions. Use a colored pencil or marker to underline concrete or key information for each question above.

Use the right column to note words and information that summarize what you discovered while underlining. Comments might include, *I produce the best work in the morning!* or *Walking helps me write better!*

When you're done, make a list of the situations and practices using the categories in the example below. You can also add your own categories.

Example: Best Possible Situations and Practices

What: If your best writing sessions are spent working on a specific kind of project, record it here. E.g., book chapter, short story, speech.

For: Note whether your best sessions were for someone else or for yourself.

Deadline: Did your best sessions come with or without a deadline? Did you work better generously ahead of or up against a deadline?

When: Record your most productive times of the day to write.

Where: Where were your best places to work and their characteristics. E.g., Is it a public place or somewhere in your home? Are you alone or with people?

External: What external elements helped you write? E.g., You were working towards a deadline or you were completing a project for a class.

Internal: What internal elements aided your productivity? E.g., You were in a good mood or you felt engaged by the material.

Practices, habits, tools: What practices did you use when you wrote most? What practices did you use to overcome writing blocks and other challenges?

Note: Many of the practices and habits that helped you write, overcome blocks, and plow through challenges are called power-ups. You'll be taking a look at this information in a later quest (see "25. Discover Favorite Power-ups" on page 89). For now, you might want to star any practice that boosts your energy.

Game Play Tips
- When you're finished, take the above information and create a personal how-to guide for writing well—a handbook of best practices. Don't overthink this! Create a quick list of your top tools or practices and post it where you can review it and use it regularly.
- If you have difficulty remembering your best writing sessions, consider keeping a writing journal. After each writing session, note what worked and what didn't work. Reflect on some of the prompts above, collecting information on the places, habits, and practices that work best for you. After a few of these sessions, review them and create your list of best practices.
- If your inner critic shows up and reminds you of all the times you failed at writing, the sessions that didn't work, and the projects you haven't finished—take notes. You can use this information in the quest "23. Find Wisdom in Weaknesses" on page 83.

For the Win
Hopefully this quest helped you see what practices work best for you. Most of the quests in this book have the same goal: helping you discover the practices that make you a happy, productive writer. As you work through the book, feel free to add any of the tools you find to your handbook of best practices. For now, celebrate that you are a creative who has developed your own best practices—yay you!

22. RECOGNIZE YOUR STRENGTHS

Identify a person's strengths. Define outcomes that play to those strengths. Find a way to count, rate or rank those outcomes. And then let the person run.

– Marcus Buckingham

One of my teaching mentors gave me this advice about managing a challenging class, "Encourage and reward the positives. Even if they're small."

In school, I learned key critical thinking skills. They've helped me earn degrees, master new topics, and write books. These same critical thinking skills support me in helping clients overcome obstacles and write more. But sometimes, my analyzing gets me stuck in a critical mindset. Instead of writing, I analyze every single problem and misstep in my writing and life. I can barely get a few words on paper before my inner critic is launching an attack.

After learning how important it is for students to hear what they're doing right, I realized that those of us engaged in the challenging task of writing have the same need. I wondered: What might happen if we paid attention to what went well and did more of that? What if we noticed, encouraged, and rewarded our own positive steps forward? And what if we recruited our strengths to support us when we were struggling with a task?

My guess? Noticing the positive would help us write more and do it with ease.

Here's an example from my work with students at the library. One of my students struggles with the technical skills of writing and, because of that, he's often reluctant to join us at the Dream Keeper's writing table. But this young man loves to draw. Once, when we were writing about how we'd change our community for the better, I invited him to draw his idea. He dove in, sketching out the details of how he'd have police officers collect guns from criminals. I asked him to write a few sentences about what he'd told me. After drawing and explaining his idea, he easily wrote the sentences. Of course, his sentences still had some technical errors— but I could see his pride in finishing an assignment. I'm certain this student will approach his next assignment with a little less fear—partly because he knows he can organize his ideas by drawing them.

This quest will help you notice what you do well—and then use those skills to level up your writing life.

The Quest

In the last quest, "21. Discern Your Best Practices" on page 77, you examined your best working sessions and noted many of the practices, habits, and tools that help you write. In this quest, you will examine the data from that quest and search for your strengths.

What is a strength? A strength might be a trait like curiosity; a skill like research, drafting, or editing; or a knowledge base, like health.

This quest might be challenging. It requires a lot of work—thinking through best writing sessions, identifying strengths, and imagining how they might support us in our writing life. It would be easy to skip the quest and "wing it" instead. But that would be a mistake. The beauty of this quest is that discovering your strengths and then learning to apply them will help you work in a way that is most helpful for you, your habits, and rhythms.

Step One: Record

Take your journal to a coffee shop, library, or park bench. Pull out the notes on your best writing sessions and reflect on the following questions. When you jot down your answers, use as much detail as possible.

- What writing or other creative tasks do I find to be easy or do well (or both)? (Examples of tasks: organize ideas, interview sources, write anecdotes, tell stories, persuade readers, research, write rough drafts, revise, etc.)
- When was I engaged with my work? What project was I working on at the time? What task was I doing? What were some of the circumstances around my work? (E.g., was I working alone or with others?)
- When did I feel most energized by my work? What project was I working on? What task was I doing? What were some of the circumstances around my work?

Step Two: Analyze

Review your answers to the above questions and reflect:

- What practices add to my productivity? (Please define productivity in any way that works for you: writing more words, beginning and completing pieces, putting in a certain amount of time, etc.)
- What practices or situations challenged my ability to be productive?
- What traits emerge as my strengths? If you have trouble putting your strengths into words, search online for lists of "strengths" or "character traits."

Step Three: Transform

Change happens when we allow what we do well to transform our writing and lives.

- Based on the above data and analysis, what kinds of projects would you like to do more of? Less of?
- How can your strengths and positive practices improve your writing sessions or other creative work?
- How can these strengths and practices support you in overcoming your blocks or challenges?

Game Play Tips

- If your inner critic shows up and natters on about your weaknesses, take notes. You can use this information in "23. Find Wisdom in Weaknesses" on page 83.
- If you get stuck, take a look at your secret identity. What are his or her character traits or strengths? How do they relate to you and your strengths?
- You may have difficulty looking at writing experiences and seeing strengths in what you do or how you do it. Part of that is because we don't value our own daily habits, it's "just what we do." It might be helpful to ask a close friend or colleague to help you find the strengths in the way you do your work as well as in the work you do.

For the Win

Your strengths are evident in everything you do—from cleaning your house to writing a book. But most of us review our life in order to uncover our weaknesses. We think that if we can get a handle on our faults and fix them, we will be more successful. In doing that, we often ignore our own superpowers—the strengths that we use to make a difference in the world. But today you changed all that. You reviewed your own life and named your strengths. Now it will be easier for you to remember and use them.

23. FIND WISDOM IN WEAKNESSES

*Never forget what you are, for surely the world will not. Make it
your strength. Then it can never be your weakness. Armour yourself
in it, and it will never be used to hurt you.*

– George R.R. Martin

In the last two quests, you've reviewed your most productive writing
sessions and uncovered your best practices and writing strengths. No
doubt your inner critic showed up and reminded you of every challenging writing experience you've had. Hopefully you took notes! Instead of
dismissing the inner critic and ignoring our weaknesses, we can learn
from them.

Knowing and understanding our weaknesses can help us in two distinct ways. First, our weaknesses often point to our strengths. For example,
a client of mine had difficulty concentrating on his writing project after
hearing about a colleague who was ill. He couldn't focus. Instead, he
checked social media and his email every hour or so for updates. When
we spoke, he worried about his poor discipline. I noted that this experience had uncovered his strengths: empathy, deep care and concern for
others, and even curiosity. He could use all of these strengths in service
of his writing. For more information on how to use our weaknesses to
uncover strengths, see "24. Uncover Secret Super Powers" on page 86.

Second, knowing our weaknesses can help us help ourselves. If we
can identify when we are tempted to be distracted, then we can also set
ourselves up for success. This quest will help us do just that.

The Quest

In "21. Discern Your Best Practices" on page 77, you recalled your best
writing sessions and recorded information about them including the place
and time you were working. For this quest, you'll recall your most difficult
writing sessions and record the same details, including what helped you to
either abandon or rescue the writing session.

Record

In your journal, write about three of your least productive writing sessions.
As in "Discern Your Best Practices," write only on the left side of the page
so you can use the right side to make notes in the next phase of the quest.
Make sure to note the following:

What: What were you working on?

When: What time of day were you working?

Where: What was the setting like?

External: What external elements distracted you from writing? (E.g., interruptions, noise, social media)

Internal: What internal elements distracted you from your work? (E.g., negative feelings, ill health)

Accomplished: What did you accomplish despite the distractions? What practices did you use to try to overcome distractions and write?

Struggled: What did you struggle with the most?

Reflect

Review the records of your least productive writing times. Use a colored pencil or marker to underline concrete or key information for each question above.

Now use the right column to note words and information that summarize what you discovered while underlining. Comments might include, *Can't write when the kids or dogs are around!* or *I need to take a day off after finishing a big project.*

Note Best Practices

When you're done with the first two steps, make a list of the habits and practices that will help you avoid or overcome difficult writing sessions. Like in "21. Discern Your Best Practices" on page 77, you might choose to include categories of the times, places, situations, and practices that make it easier to write. You might also include a list of potential warnings that will help you notice challenging situations and shift course.

Game Play Tips

- If you have trouble recalling difficult writing sessions, complete this quest after you have a tough writing session or two.
- Check in with your allies (see "26. Identify Your Allies" on page 91) for additional information. What do they recall as being your toughest challenges?
- Remember that the point of this quest is to learn what doesn't work so you can address it. The goal is to find a solution—not to beat up on yourself.

For the Win

As an athlete, I've noticed that developing strength comes both from building on what I am doing well and from correcting my missteps and weaknesses. In the past few quests and again in the next one, you've been able to do both! You're on your way to becoming a creative superstar!

24. UNCOVER SECRET SUPER POWERS

Did you know, you were born as the first, and the last and the best and the only one of your kind, and that eccentricity is the first sign of giftedness? These are two of the crone truths I have to offer you.

– Clarissa Pinkola Estes

I recently had a conversation with a three-year-old boy wearing a cape. He told me about his secret super powers (I'm not allowed to share them with you). I don't know about you, but on most days a few super powers (not to mention the cape) would come in mighty handy for writing.

Author and Jungian psychoanalyst Dr. Clarissa Pinkola Estes says that we can find our giftedness (i.e., our secret super powers) inside our eccentricities. Often people criticize us for the very thing that makes us unique and exceptional. She encourages people to list everything they've been ridiculed or criticized for—and then look for the gift hiding under it.

When I did the exercise, I remembered something a colleague said to me in grad school, "It's not that you lack intelligence. It's just that you're not serious enough." At the time, I felt criticized and hurt. I ranted in my head: *What did she mean by not serious enough? I'll show her. I can be just as serious as the rest of them.* But no matter how hard I tried, I could not hide or lose my sense of humor.

Perhaps that classmate was offering constructive criticism, but at the time I heard it as pure judgment. Years later, I can see my strengths inside her critique: *You are playful. You are funny. Keep that at the heart of your work.* When I'm stuck with writing, I can always write forward by using my secret super power: my sense of humor.

In this quest, you'll mine uncomfortable experiences for signs of your brilliance.

The Quest

As humans, we tend to remember the negative messages and experiences more easily than we recall the kind words people say. We might even dismiss their words as a fluke. This is called the negativity bias or negativity effect. Ruminating on these negative experiences can cause us to feel bad about ourselves.

In this quest, we will be recalling some of these messages but for a better purpose. Instead of perseverating on the criticisms we've received and beating up on ourselves for our faults, we will be looking at these critiques for signs of our brilliance. That doesn't mean this task will be easy. When we review our difficult past experiences, we feel them all over again. But remember: this quest is about naming and claiming who you are. No one else gets to define you.

Take a deep breath. Start by recording the criticisms you've received. Then list the eccentricities that your coworkers, friends, and family complain about. These might come up when someone is reviewing your work. It could also be something you criticize yourself for. Jot down anything that others have said or you've thought. Note the stories people tell about you that annoy you.

Once you have a list of criticisms, dig underneath each one to find the hints of your genius or secret super power that lurks inside each eccentricity. Here are some examples:

- When one of my clients finds a bruise or gets a cold, she worries about all the exotic ailments she could have. I believe her worrying is just one manifestation of her brilliant imagination.
- A student of mine has a habit of trying to negotiate deals instead of doing his work. When he heard about a local poetry contest, he proposed, "If you help me write a great poem, I will share my winnings with you. Like a tip." I see this as a sign of his creativity.
- I've heard people criticize professional writers for taking an assignment for one outlet, revising or recasting it, and then selling it to other publications. But this is genius! Much like cooks who don't waste any part of a chicken, these writers use their leftover information for more articles and earn more money.

Game Play Tips

- Look at personal habits that others might find annoying or endearing. For example, I like to chat with strangers. My children get irritated by this habit, but it comes in handy when I need to interview someone for an article.
- If you have difficulty remembering your eccentricities, ask a close friend or family member to offer ideas. (It will take some bravery, it's not easy to hear what other people find challenging about us—but go for it. You just might discover that you are beloved for your kookiness.)
- Consider the traits your inner critic pounces on you for. Is it possible that these are actually super powers?
- Take a look at the weaknesses you uncovered for the last quest. They might hold clues for your secret super powers as well.
- For more information on the Negativity bias, check out the quest "38. Examine Your Thoughts" on page 128. For help in turning around negative thoughts and messages, check out "40. Lasso of Truth" on page 132 and "47. Reframe Blocks" on page 151.

For the Win

This might be one of the more difficult quests. But once you've learned to look at criticisms for signs of your brilliance, you'll see all future negative messages in a new light. And of course, now that you know your secret super powers, you can use them to overcome fear, doubt, and writer's block and finish that writing project!

25. DISCOVER FAVORITE POWER-UPS

Renew energy, revive strength.

– Lailah Gifty Akita

When we play a video game, power-ups provide extra abilities or add a benefit. When Pac-Man eats a power pellet—a large flashing dot near each corner of the game board—his enemies turn deep blue, reverse direction, and he can eat them. But when the ghosts flash white, the player knows that Pac-Man's special power is fading. The ghosts will soon become dangerous again.

In real life, power-ups function much like water stops in a marathon. We need them to perform well. In the book *SuperBetter*, author Jane McGonigal defines power-ups as "any positive action you can take easily that creates a quick moment of pleasure, strength, courage, or connection for you."[23] She notes that power-ups can boost our resilience in many areas of our life: social, physical, emotional, and mental. For many of us, power-ups like exercise, healthy food, and connecting with others support us in getting through the day. For writers, power-ups boost energy, help us blast through writer's block or simple exhaustion, and work through the challenging parts. Power-ups can mean the difference between quitting and succeeding.

In writing lore, power-ups have been portrayed as unhealthy and even illegal habits. T.S. Eliot took Benzedrine (an amphetamine) every morning and Seconal or another sleep aid every night to go to sleep. While writing *The Power and the Glory*, Graham Greene took on a second project—a thriller called *The Confidential Agent*. In order to finish both books quickly, he took a Benzedrine tablet at morning and noon. Science fiction writer Philip K. Dick used hallucinogenics and speed-like drugs to pump out fiction fast.

Other writers confess to habits that are fully legal and equally addicting. We use caffeine to get going in the morning. When our energy lags, we boost it with coffee, chocolate, and sugar-laden substances (donuts!). The extroverts among us—I know you're out there—take to the internet like workers visit the water cooler, hoping for encouragement, camaraderie, or concrete information.

And those on the wannabe list—we wannabe writers but we're still working out how to do it—often wait for the elusive inspiration power-up to hit and ignite our writing sessions.

After writing professionally for more than 20 years, I recognize that certain types of power-ups have helped me write more than 15 books and many articles. And although I love coffee and chocolate and pie, none of these substances have helped me write more. What power-ups have worked? Simple tools like exercise, journaling, and accountability have given me the energy boosts that keep me focused and productive.

In this quest, you'll examine your own life to discover your most helpful power-ups.

The Quest

Power-ups can help us feel energized, attentive, witty, powerful, calm, happy, healthy, and strong. Consider what helps you access these emotions or states of being. Make lists of any experiences, exercises, activities, places, songs, quotes, mantras, advice, photos, movies, videos, habits, food, memories, volunteer activities, people, or anything else that boosts your energy and supports you in writing.

If you've been working through this section in order, you've already examined most and least productive writing sessions as well as detecting your strengths and weaknesses. Take a look at the information you uncovered in each of these quests and note any power-ups that you regularly use to renew your energy before or during your writing session.

Take a look at the practices you use to restore energy in other parts of your life. What do you do at work when you're feeling burned out or restless but you have a project due that day? How do you recoup your energy when you come home from a long day at work and need to cook dinner? How do you gather energy when you're tired and need to care for children, a friend, or pets? Add these power-ups to the list.

Game Play Tips

- Connect with a friend or writing colleague and ask what helps them to write when they feel stuck or confused. Swap tips.
- Review the "Power-up List" on page 237 at the end of this book and note which ones you already use and which you'd like to try. Add your favorite power-ups to the list.
- Post a list of your power-ups where you can see them throughout the day. Next time you feel stuck, try a power-up.
- Commit to using at least one power-up a day.

For the Win

Now that you have your super duper list of power-up tools, you can find the power to focus and write whenever you need to. When you feel stuck or uninspired, ask: would a power-up help? Then check your list and use one!

26. IDENTIFY YOUR ALLIES

*This is what we can all do to nourish and strengthen one another:
listen to one another very hard, ask hard questions, too, send one
another away to work again, and laugh in all the right places.*

– Nancy Mairs

As a spokesperson for Weight Watchers, Oprah Winfrey promotes one
of the cornerstone secrets for successful weight loss: connecting. She said,
"The journey is even better when you take it together."

Neuroscientist Moran Cerf said that we can reduce stress, increase
happiness, and make better choices by connecting with the right people.[24]
Cerf based this theory on three research-supported concepts. First, we
make hundreds of decisions a day, from when to get up to what to eat
to how we'll spend our time, and the act of choosing drains our energy.
Second, when we make choices, we're not always rational. Our biases,
emotions, and social connections cloud our judgment. In other words,
when it comes to choosing whether or not to have dessert, we might be
swayed by our belief that hard work needs to be rewarded or by a friend's
encouragement to indulge. Finally, we often make decisions based on
what the people around us do.

We choose wisely when we surround ourselves with people who make
good choices.[25] Motivational speaker Jim Rohn said it this way: "You are
the average of the five people you spend the most time with."

Choosing healthy companions can affect our writing life as well as
what we eat or how much we exercise. Psychology professor Robert
Boice[26] examined the habits of productive and unproductive faculty
writers. He found that writers who belonged to peer writing groups
received the following benefits:

- Maintained momentum to complete a project
- Produced more work
- Developed more creative ideas
- Improved the quality of their writing
- Identified sources for publication

Wow!

In game language, the people you connect with are your allies. This
quest provides you with multiple options for connecting with potential
allies. Try out a few of them and measure which has the most positive
impact on your writing life.

The Quest

Review the following models for connecting. Under each category note your current allies and star the types of connecting that might work best for you right now.

Friends and Family

The people you connect with regularly can be some of your best allies. Friends and family members can help you celebrate your successes, cheer you up when you're struggling, and support you through it all. People who are also working on creative projects can be especially helpful allies.

Coach

A coach will help you vision, set goals, create a plan, overcome blocks, and stay accountable. You might hire a coach for help with a single challenge or to be an accountability partner for the whole process.

Accountability Partner

An accountability partner can help you maintain momentum in achieving your goals. In this sort of relationship, it's helpful if both people are working toward achieving a goal and need accountability.

Pro Tip: When you're both working on a writing project, it can help to make a deadline pact. Promise that by a certain date you will each write a set number of words, finish a project, or complete a portion of a manuscript. To make it more fun and easier to succeed, make a bet. Perhaps the loser can treat the winner to dinner!

Support Group

For years, I've met with small networking and support groups for accountability. When I wanted to quit, these connections have helped me to leap forward. During these meetings, we ask questions like:

- What are you creating?
- What do you hope to be creating?
- What's working?
- What do you need help with?

Critique Group

Professional writers study great writing—and know what works and what doesn't work. When you invite other writers to read and critique your writing, you expand your understanding of good writing. And, you learn about your blind spots. From complex comments on structure and voice to technical lessons on commas and run-on sentences, a good critique can strengthen your writing. Plus, having a critique group often provides you with the deadline you need to finish a draft of your work.

Class

When you cannot make progress even with the help of a coach or coaching group, you might consider taking a class. With the help of an instructor and colleagues, you'll receive assignments, due dates, feedback, and accountability. In addition, paying a fee can sometimes help us work harder.

Find and Connect

After reviewing and reflecting on the above possibilities for connecting, you will have an idea of what kind of connection would work best for you at this time. If you're developing a writing habit or starting a writing project, it might be most helpful to get a coach or accountability partner to cheer you on and help you when you hit roadblocks. Or maybe you're feeling ready to submit your work but would like some feedback on your work—then it might be time to connect with an editor or critique group.

Once you know what kind of connection you want, brainstorm people who might make good allies. If you get stuck, ask current allies who they would recommend. Search online for additional opportunities—coaches, critique groups, and classes. Then connect!

Game Play Tips

- When you try a connecting tool, track your progress. Choose a goal you want to accomplish—perhaps increasing your weekly word count, discovering tools to overcome writer's block, or finishing a project. Note your progress on the goal as well as how the group or partnership affects you. Does it increase or decrease your energy? Do you feel more or less confident? This reflection will help you find connections that work!
- Give each connecting tool time to work. One coaching session or one critique group session can be helpful, but several can be transformational. It takes time to develop trust, and transformational relationships are built on a foundation of trust.
- You may need to try a few coaches, accountability partners, or groups before you find one that suits you.

For the Win

Creating can be a challenging game. Writers work alone for months or years to produce a product they're satisfied with. But that's just the opening match. Whether we sell our product to a publisher, packager, or directly to a reader, the process can be a lengthy and frustrating experience, filled with rejection and stumbling blocks. The successful creatives find and connect with allies. We cheer each other on, not only when we cross finish lines but also when we're starting a new project, facing challenges, or feeling discouraged. When we have allies, we're winners no matter what happens.

27. NAME YOUR VILLAINS

A great hero is nothing without a great villain. Honestly, who cares about the kid picking up a sword and going on an adventure if there isn't some evildoer waiting at the end of the trail? It's the villain that makes the hero; the role of the "bad guy" is the most important of them all.

– GamesRadar Staff

What's a story without a good villain? Readers of the Harry Potter books love bonding over our shared dislike for Lord Voldemort, Draco Malfoy, and the Dementors. So while we play for the epic wins and we hope to best our opponents and the game, we also want to take on the villains. And when we confront the villains and win, the struggle makes the success seem even more delicious!

In this quest, you'll identify and name your villains. Yikes—why? Doesn't naming them give them power over us? On the contrary. Villains thrive in the dark. They do best when we don't know who they are and what they can do. In our imaginations, the villains become like the all-powerful Wizard of Oz, able to do great things. In the light of day, we see that they are smaller than we envisioned and less powerful than we'd imagined.

The Quest

In previous quests, you examined your most productive and difficult writing sessions. You identified what worked and what didn't work. Review those journal entries and evaluate them for anything that might qualify as one of your villains, like the inner critic or distractions. Create a list of villains, with a short description for each.

Some of the items on your list—like the inner critic—sound like a villain. But you may need to name some of the forces you battle with. Create a section in your journal or game playbook that names and describes each villain. If you have any ideas about how to defeat this villain, add that too. Here are some examples.

Doubt Dragon

The hot, fiery breath of the Doubt Dragon appears on the writer's neck and murmurs, "Seriously? How will this help? You can do everything they do and still fail." The Doubt Dragon collects these negative messages from the writer and their people and breathes them on the creator at just the right moments.

How to defeat it: Douse that Dragon and his nasty fire with the cold water of truth! Question every doubt. Dismiss it with facts. Crush it with information about the moments you have overcome doubts and succeeded.

Lizard Brain

The lizard brain lives to protect us from harm but cannot judge what fear is real or imagined. So, whenever we step out of the lizard's comfort zone, even to do something good, it freaks out.

How to defeat it: Remind your Lizard Brain that you're only dreaming, not doing—and keep dreaming. Eat something. (Lizard Brain feeds on your hunger.) If the Lizard Brain really freaks out, do an activity that engages your thinking brain, like a word puzzle or Sudoku. The Lizard Brain will calm down, and you can vision again!

Squirrel Brain

Sometimes called Monkey Mind, Squirrel Brain waits for you to make plans—and then pounces on a shiny new idea or project or event. As soon as you've written your goal—or maybe even when you just begin to think about it—Squirrel Brain will remind you of the 9 other book ideas you should also be working on, the friends who need you, the 64 things in your house that must be done, and a few more tasks on social media, as well. Pro Tip: Squirrel Brain also gets very active when you write.

How to defeat it: Create a file in your computer or set aside a section of your journal to jot down any ideas or projects that Squirrel Brain worries you'll forget. Then get back to work on writing your goal or writing or whatever else you've set your mind to!

Game Play Tips
- Use online villain name generators to help name your villains.
- Check out the descriptions of comic book villains for help when you are trying to find, name, and describe villains.
- As you work through the quests in the next few sections of the book, you will discover many new villains and uncover tools for defeating them! Don't worry if you don't have a big bag of tricks to defeat the villains right now—you'll be compiling a long list of badass weapons.

For the Win

According to the quote at the beginning of this quest, the hero needs the villain. On my difficult days, when I am struggling to write and worrying that I'm a fraud, I feel like the villains are there to prevent me from succeeding. But then I remember—we are who we are because we've battled the villains and won. Each time we make it to the page and write, we win. When we query despite our fear, we win. When we keep going when we could have quit, we win. So don't give up. Fight those villains!

28. DEVELOP A WRITING HABIT

First forget inspiration. Habit is more dependable. Habit will sustain you whether you're inspired or not. Habit will help you finish and polish your stories. Inspiration won't. Habit is persistence in practice.

– Octavia E. Butler

Wannabe writers tend to depend on inspiration to cue them to write. Unfortunately, inspiration comes most frequently while we are writing and not before. Many famous writers talked about the power of making writing a habit. In the quote above, science fiction writer Octavia Butler reminded her readers that habit sustains us long after inspiration has disappeared. When novelist Haruki Murakami is writing a book, he sticks to a strict schedule of rising early, writing for 5-6 hours, and then going for a run.

Flannery O'Connor also believed in the habit of writing, saying: "I'm a full-time believer in writing habits... Of course you have to make your habits in this conform to what you can do. I write only about two hours every day because that's all the energy I have, but I don't let anything interfere with those two hours, at the same time and the same place."[27]

In his book, *The Power of Habit*, Charles Duhigg gave the concept of habit a structure with three distinct steps: cue, practice, reward."[28] This habit loop might be as simple as brushing your teeth:

- Cue: It's bedtime.
- Practice: Brush teeth
- Reward: Ohhh! My mouth feels fresh and clean.

In order to succeed at writing, we can adopt the habit loop and use it as a tool to make our own writing a habit. When we do that, it increases our productivity. In this quest, you will determine your cue, practice, and reward and then put it into place.

Quest
Once again, we will examine our lives for the practices that help us. It may be useful to review "21. Discern Your Best Practices" on page 77 for information about current and past writing habits.

Find a Cue
When J. K. Rowling was writing the first Harry Potter book, the minute her daughter fell asleep (cue), she'd take off for the café and write (habit). Keith Donahue, author of *The Stolen Child* and *Angels of Destruction*, wrote

both novels by hand on his subway commute to and from work. His cue was getting on the train. If you schedule when and where you will write, you will know your cue. I've nurtured my writing habit by creating a morning ritual. Before I check Facebook or email, I take a look at my writing task of the day, left on my bullet journal next to my computer, and write. Once I've put in my writing time, I reward myself with a trip to Facebook or a walk around the block.

Design Your Practice
Know when, where and what you will create. If you are writing and fear the blank page, do "30. Know the What" on page 102. It will show you how using a prewriting exercise can eliminate the fear of the blank page. If you need research materials like books or special supplies, gather them together before your work session.

Plan Your Reward
For many writers, the effort of having written feels like a reward in itself. Whew! But if that's not quite enough for you, one way to keep your butt in the chair is to promise yourself a delicious reward. Famous writers have rewarded themselves in unique ways: Anthony Burgess used the Martini Method. When he had completed his word count, he would relax with a dry martini and enjoy the rest of the day with an easy conscience, and normally in a bar. I suggest more healthy rewards. A walk in the park. An hour reading a good book. A trip to the library. See "25. Discover Favorite Power-ups" on page 89 for more ideas.

Game Play Tips
- Mine the past to discover what cues and rewards you used during your most productive writing sessions.
- If you have difficulty finding a cue that works, piggyback on an existing habit, the tasks you do every day or week. Even when you're swamped with work or overwhelmed with tasks, you do a few things every single day: get up, brush your teeth, eat breakfast, check email, take a snack break, go to bed. You also do a few things every week at the same time: go to yoga class, pick up kids from school, or visit a family member in the nursing home. Take one of these constants and attach writing to it, either before or after.
- Review and revise. Try out a cue, practice, and reward for the next few writing sessions. At the end of each session, note what worked and what didn't. After several sessions with a single cue, review your practice and revise anything that isn't working well.

For the Win

We don't need elaborate cues or rewards to get to our creative projects and complete them. And once we know what cues work for us and practice honoring them, we'll be well on our way to creating a writing habit, which is the best way to increase productivity and finish projects!

29. TAKE SMALL STEPS

When asked, "How do you write?" I invariably answer, "one word at a time."

– Stephen King

I've been meaning to clean the basement for some time. Every week, I dutifully scribble, "clean the basement" on my to-do list. And every week, I look at that entry and my stomach sinks. Before I pick up a single box, I'm overwhelmed.

Of course, that's not the only thing on my to-do list that sends my stomach into back flips. Every week for some time now, I've also written: "revise the novel" and "write new book."

You can guess how much progress I've made on both the basement and the books: zero. Here's why: my brain cannot cope with the thought of doing a huge task like "clean the basement." I might as well have added to my to-do list, "reverse climate change."

Lots of coaches talk about the Big Hairy Audacious Goal (BHAG). Write the book and clean the basement count as BHAGs. And here's what I've learned over many years of coaching: having a big hairy audacious goal is a huge hurdle to accomplishing anything.

Humans do not do well with giant steps or drastic changes. Why do you think so many of us fail at these lifestyle-changing diets? The fear part of our brain freaks out. Instead of cleaning the basement, revising the novel, or eliminating sugar, we'll do just about anything to avoid that big, scary goal.

Think about your own writing life and tackling that big project you've wanted to take on for years. Or consider cleaning out one of the places you've packed to the gills with stuff (the attic, garage, car trunk). Did your stomach just sink a bit? Maybe you had a sudden urge to eat chocolate or get a root canal, anything to avoid "the big task."

Don't worry. Take a deep breath. I have a solution for you: take a small step. According to Robert Maurer, author of *One Small Step Can Change Your Life: The Kaizen Way*, we avoid that sinking feeling by taking absurdly small steps toward our goals.[29] Instead of filling our to-do list with big chunks like, "write book" or "clean house," we list tiny actions like "write a paragraph about taking small steps."

This quest will help you divide a big goal into small steps and tackle them, one tiny turtle step at a time.

The Quest
Use your journal to work through the following steps.

Step One

Choose a current project and break down the tasks into absurdly tiny steps. So instead of "write book" try something like:

- Brainstorm chapter topics
- Choose a chapter topic
- Brainstorm ideas for topic
- Write a sentence explaining the topic

Step Two

This week, when you schedule writing time, note the step (or steps) you will work on during each time slot.

Step Three

Tackle a single small step at a time during each writing slot.

At the end of a week or two, reflect on how small steps have supported your writing progress.

Game Play Tips

- Pay attention to how you feel as you record or work on each step. If you feel overwhelmed, blocked, or panicked, the step may be too big. Break down the task into even smaller steps. So "write an hour each day" might become "write fifteen minutes each day" or "write for five minutes about the first session with my running coach."
- Small steps are a power-up, too. They're also a great tool for defeating the lizard part of your brain, who freaks out whenever you take a big step (see "27. Name Your Villains" on page 94). Take an even smaller step, and the lizard brain will calm down.
- Call on a power animal for inspiration and ideas. When it comes to taking small steps, it helps to have a power animal to get inspired and learn how to move forward. Think about spiders spinning webs, ants carrying food back to their nest, or a turtle foraging for food. All of these creatures tackle their projects at their own speed. What can you learn from their habits? How might they inspire you? Use their work as an example or inspiration and take even smaller steps toward your goal.

For the Win

Often movies or television shows portray the stories of people who took dramatic action. When we compare ourselves to them, we may feel like we can never measure up. But just because the movie doesn't show all of the small steps the protagonist took to achieve her goal, including the multiple missteps, doesn't mean they didn't happen. Victory is achieved one small step at a time. Embrace it!

30. KNOW THE WHAT

The blank page is God's way of letting us know how hard it is to be God.

– G.K. Chesterton

Many writers have talked about their fear of the blank page. But there's a perfect solution to facing the blank page: don't.

Prewriting—brainstorming or mapping out ideas before writing—eliminates the blank page. This tool comes from my training with the National Writing Project. Students write better if they can start with some sort of prewriting. You will, too.

Before we write the paper or the scene, we jot down our thoughts, without any pressure to get it right. The process of exploring the idea in writing can help us identify our core ideas, develop illustrations and details to enrich our writing, and organize our thoughts. When it's time to write, we no longer worry about the blank page—we have a map to follow. This quest offers you several tools to try as prewriting tools.

The Quest

Knowing what you will write each day—even jotting a few notes about it, will help you write with ease. On the day before your next scheduled writing session, choose a small step to complete during that session. In your journal or computer document, note your topic.

Then brainstorm how you might write about the topic in any way that works for you. Here are some possible tools[30] for prewriting. Use one or combine several together for your prewriting.

Mind map. Write your topic in the center of a piece of paper and, like spokes on a bicycle, record any anecdotes, facts, data, or examples that will help you write about the topic.

List. Create a list of potential topics, stories, ideas, and more.

Free-write. Write anything that comes to mind about the topic.

Ask questions. Formulate questions about the topic including what you want to know about it, how you will present it, or anything else that helps you move forward.

Draw pictures. For people who feel more comfortable using images, drawing pictures about an aspect of your topic can help you move into writing. Some people use pictures when they create a mind map.

Create a rough outline. Some people like to have a map for moving forward with their project. Developing a rough outline can provide that road map.

Create a to-do list with tiny steps. An outline can also be thought of as a big to-do list, with the steps written in order of presentation. For this to-do list, write anything that comes to mind—and don't worry about the order.

Use a prewriting chart. For a scene it might have categories like: characters, setting, main conflict, emotional conflict, etc. For a nonfiction article, it might identify: main point, central ideas, supporting data, anecdotes, details, etc.

After 10-15 minutes of prewriting, put away your work until your writing session. Your subconscious will continue to work on the topic and when you get to your writing session, you'll have no trouble writing!

Game Play Tips

- Play with various types of prewriting methods until you find one or two that work for you. Know that the prewriting tools that work may vary with the type of project you're working on.
- The quest suggests prewriting the day before your writing session. Feel free to adapt this—and see what happens. Prewrite each morning for that evening's writing session or simply prewrite at the beginning of your writing time.
- If you prewrite and still don't know how to begin the section you're working on, don't sweat it. Set aside that prewriting for a future writing session. Take a look at your list of potential topics and select a topic seems the most engaging. Brainstorm ideas and try writing on that. If neither of these tools work, take a break. The solution may appear to you in the middle of the night, while folding laundry, or at tomorrow's writing session.

For the Win

Writers have taken drastic measures to overcome their fear of the blank page—including taking drugs and consuming large amounts of alcohol. Prewriting will eliminate fear better than drugs, wine, and chocolate! And there are many types of prewriting tools to try. If brainstorming doesn't work, then try mind mapping or making a list of questions. At some point, you'll be able to start writing.

31. CLUSTER TASKS

Progress isn't made by early risers. It's made by lazy men trying to find easier ways to do something.

– Robert A. Heinlein

My family enjoys freshly baked treats, so I regularly whip up a batch of something yummy. During the holiday season, I set aside an afternoon to bake. In just a few hours, we make dozens of cookies, several loaves of sweet bread, and a batch of hot air candy. When I reflect on my baking sessions, I'm surprised that while the holiday baking afternoons are just a bit longer than my regular baking sessions, I'm able to produce more.

The trick? Clustering. When it comes to baking—and many other big projects—getting set up and started for a single task takes the same amount of work as getting set up for doing that same task multiple times. During holiday baking, once I've dragged out the mixer, pans, and ingredients, the bulk of the heavy work is done. All I have to do is follow the recipes to mix, bake, and repeat.

When people say that they multitask, they often mean that they're doing multiple things at once. But multitasking is really switching tasks, often quite frequently. You've been there: write a sentence, check email, write another sentence, check Facebook, research, write another sentence, check Twitter, and repeat. That's insane!

Clustering tasks sounds fancy but it's really nothing more than grouping together similar items on our to-do list. This quest will help you to focus on a single type of task at once.

The Quest

The goal of this quest is to get more focused time to write. For that reason, it helps to begin by clustering the tasks that tend to interrupt your writing time.

For me, that's Facebook and email. I'm often tempted to check in with both at the beginning of the day—just so I don't miss out on any important business responsibilities. Unfortunately, my quick check in often takes an hour, and by the time I finish, I've lost half of my writing time.

Now I cluster email and social media time during the late morning—so that I still respond to business requests early in the day, but don't lose my writing time. I've let my clients and colleagues know my schedule, so they won't expect me to respond to email too quickly.

Step One: Identify and Cluster Tasks

List all of the tasks you do and consider how you could cluster them together. For example, if you regularly check email and social media throughout the day, you could cluster those activities and set aside time to do them. I also block out time for writing, in person and phone meetings, marketing, and more.

Step Two: Schedule

Create a schedule for the next day or week, blocking out time to do your various clusters of tasks. Review the schedule and ask, "Is there anything else I can cluster together?"

Step Three: Reflect

After a day or week of clustering tasks, reflect on how working on projects in blocks of time helped you to get more done. If it didn't help you, check to see if you need to make each time block more specific. For example, if you have clustered social media and email time together and you didn't get enough done, you may need to separate each into its own time block.

Game Play Tip

- Because the goal of this task is to get more time to do your creative work, make sure you block out time to write or make art and to do any other tasks related to your creative work.
- Once you've done this for a day or week, try regularly blocking out your schedule, clustering like tasks together.
- Know that it will take some discipline to design a schedule and stick to it. You will need to ignore texts and emails while you write or perform other tasks.

For the Win

Clustering tasks has allowed me to work guilt free. I no longer worry about answering emails or completing jobs for clients because I know I will get to them at the time I set aside to do them. This has helped clear my mind of its spinning list of responsibilities and focus on writing.

32. AUTOMATE DECISIONS

You will never change your life until you change something you do daily. The secret of your success is found in your daily routine.

– John C. Maxwell

At a conference, I heard a speaker instruct the audience to list their habitual tasks on their to-do lists so that they could experience the joy of crossing off items like brushing their teeth, showering, and eating. When was the last time you forgot to brush your teeth? If it's a habit—you don't. For most people, certain tasks are automatic. We don't have to think about where to put our keys or what toothpaste to use—because we do the same thing every day.

And that's good. According to the work of social psychologist Roy Baumeister, we have a finite amount of mental energy for self-control. Making decisions depletes that energy, and it becomes harder for us to make good decisions. In the article "Do you suffer from Decision Fatigue?" John Tierney wrote: "The more choices you make throughout the day, the harder each one becomes for your brain, and eventually it looks for shortcuts, usually in either of two very different ways."[31] Either we make a reckless choice (*Oh sure, why not, I'll eat a bag of chocolate*) or we avoid making a choice (*You decide, honey*).

In *You: On a Diet*, Dr. Michael F. Roizen and Dr. Mehmet Oz recommended automating one's meals—eating the same rotation of healthy foods to avoid temptation.[32] Instead of pitching in cash for the office's daily pizza order, we pack one of three pre-chosen meals for lunch. Or we plan and prepare our evening meals ahead of time so we're not tempted to stop at a local fast food restaurant on the way home from work. Anytime we can automate our decisions—what to wear, what to eat, when to write—we free up brain space to think about writing.

In this quest, you'll automate some portion of your life to free up more time for your writing.

The Quest

Review the past three weeks and note any decisions that you regularly make that take a lot of time. As a freelance writer, I spend most of my days working in my yoga clothes. But a few times a month, I put on my big girl clothes to give a speech or attend a networking event. Because I rarely get dressed up, it often takes me an hour to decide what to wear. If I automated that decision, choosing ahead of time five outfits that always work, I'd save time and energy for creative endeavors.

Here are common tasks that can be easily automated:

Meals or snacks. Take a day to plan the next week's meal schedule or choose a rotation of healthy dishes to eat regularly. Instead of choosing from myriad choices for breakfast, select from three options: oatmeal, a smoothie, or an omelet. In addition, plan your snacks for the next week. You can make a list of healthy snacks or create a snack cupboard or shelf in the refrigerator.

Clothing. Instead of waking up and wondering what to wear, create a uniform for each of your main activities. For example, a work uniform might be a dress or a pair of dress pants and a button-down shirt. Each day, choose a different set. If a uniform does not work, arrange your closet by outfits and select one of those each day.

Work schedule. Every job has certain tasks that must be done regularly. Clustering those tasks and then doing them at the same time each day or week can eliminate some of the drama of deciding when to complete each task. For writers, setting aside the same time each day to write, participate in social media, or submit query letters can increase productivity. Automate as many work tasks as you can.

Email. Set aside time to decide how you're going to triage your inbox. What will you automatically delete? What will you answer quickly? What types of emails will get set aside for a longer response? What kinds of emails get filed?

Regularly used items. If you spend time searching for items you use regularly like sunglasses, keys, loyalty cards, or papers, make a plan to automate where you keep those things.

Try It

- Choose an area or a task to automate. Create a plan and put it into action.
- After 1-3 weeks, evaluate its effect on your life. Did automating the task save you time? Did it free you up to think about other tasks? If so, keep it. If not, look for another task to automate.

Game Play Tips

- Repeat this quest for any task that takes up too much time, that you worry about, or that distracts you from your work.
- We save time when we automate specific tasks and make decisions ahead of time. To increase the success of this quest, list any decision you can make in advance and then do it. This might include choosing what you'll write about, how you'll spend your free time, or, like me, what you will wear.

- Enlist your allies (see "26. Identify Your Allies" on page 91) with special skills to help you figure out what you might automate or how you could do it. For example, if you have a friend who's a great cook, you might ask them for ideas on quick, healthy meals.

For the Win

But what about spontaneity? Habits provide the security and time to entertain serendipity. When we automate the smallest decisions and schedule our pressing tasks, we open up space to think big thoughts. But this practice also prevents the schedule jams that happen when we forget to complete tasks on time. We've got extra time, and we can say yes to the surprises that show up!

33. UTILIZE TEMPLATES

Ben wished the world was organized by the Dewey decimal system.
That way you'd be able to find whatever you were looking for.

– Brian Selznick

Templates make life easier. Woodworkers use templates when they make something that's curved or contains an irregular design element. People who sew clothing and other items use patterns. As a writer and editor, I've learned to make use of templates to save time, increase quality, and simplify the writing process.

I inherited my first set of templates when I took a job as the managing editor of a quarterly periodical. My predecessor had created templates for briefing writers and sending rejection and acceptance letters. These templates made the first years of my job much easier.

As my writing and coaching practice has grown, I've developed templates for everything from follow-up emails to book proposals to podcast questions. Some of the templates are full texts, easily copied and pasted into a new document and adapted as necessary. Other templates are simply outlines, reminding me what questions I need to ask or pieces I need to fill in. For example, when I do a developmental edit of a book, I have a template with a series of questions that helps me reflect and comment on the work.

Templates can help you focus on the most important part of your work: the writing. With a template to deal with material you create regularly or to outline the rote parts of any writing project, you are free to spend your time researching possibilities, creating unique content, and shaping the narrative.

In this quest, you'll review the work you do, imagine how you could use templates, and then create key templates to ease your workload.

The Quest

Step One: Imagine the Possibilities
Templates can be useful at almost every stage of the writing process. Below is a list of documents that writers create and that could be streamlined by using a template. Check any of these that you use and believe you would benefit from using a template of it. Add any additional items to the list. Note if you will need the full text or simply an outline.

- Article outlines
- Artist statement
- Biography, in several lengths

- Blog post outlines
- Book outlines
- Book proposals
- Contracts or agreement forms
- Grant applications
- Letters of information
- Letters of recommendation
- Project guides
- Query letters
- Requests for blurbs, interviews, and more
- Writer briefings for blogs, periodicals, etc.

Step Two: Assess Your Files

You've no doubt created the documents you need at least once and probably multiple times. Review your sent mailbox, your computer's hard drive, and any external drives for documents that you can use as templates. Copy, revise to be used as a template, and save with a descriptive name, such as Query Letter Template. It might help to save these in a folder (or folders) labeled "templates" so that you know where to find them.

Step Three: Observe and Create

What? You didn't save all those emails or notes on your last project? Don't worry. You can create a new template next time you work on a project.

Each time you take on a new project, document your process and progress. Make notes about what worked, what didn't work, and what you'd like to do differently. Throughout the project, ask yourself, where would a template save me time? When you're finished with the project, create new templates to add to your template file.

Game Play Tips

- We learn as we go. Don't worry if you don't have templates for every single thing you do. Create templates as you need them. Or, take a day to develop templates that work.
- Check online for examples of templates that you can adapt for your own work.
- Connect with fellow creatives, writers, and editors and share templates.

For the Win

Imagine the time you will save once you're regularly using templates. You will have so much more time to write and play! Woot!

34. ORGANIZE YOUR OFFICE

I believe in empty spaces; they're the most wonderful thing.
– Anselm Kiefer

Most of us juggle time, tasks, and stuff. The average American home has more than 300,000 items in it. Throughout our lives, we'll spend a total of 153 days searching for misplaced or lost items. We mostly search for our phones, keys, sunglasses, and paperwork.[33]

It's hard to think big thoughts when we're dealing with finding, straightening, cleaning, and arranging our papers, books, and other junk. In Edward Hallowell's article, "Overloaded Circuits: Why Smart People Underperform," he talks about how having our circuits overloaded with information and tasks can literally cause us to lose our ability to pay attention.[34] One of his central recommendations takes on the piles of papers in our junk-filled offices: keep "a section of your workspace or desk clear at all times." (You do not need to have a neat office, just a neat section of your office.)

In this quest, you will envision the tools you need in your office, clear out what does not work, and organize what's left. If you don't have a home office, clear out whatever space you most frequently work in as well as the area where you store your supplies.

The Quest

Step One: Eliminate
Answer these questions in your journal:

- What tools and papers do you regularly need and waste time searching for?
- What stuff clutters up the spaces in between your workspace and the tools you need?
- What other items get in the way of you doing your work?

Gather supplies. You will need a timer and four containers labeled:

- *Toss.* This is a trash container.
- *Recycle.* This is for your papers.
- *Donate.* This is for books and other items that you will donate.
- *Move.* Items you want to keep in your life but not in your writing space.

Take a look at your office or workspace and get rid of anything you no longer need. Dump these items into the containers you've set out.

Step Two: Arrange

Organize your office like a kindergarten classroom. Their rooms are arranged in work zones, with places set aside for reading, playing, and making art. The tools for each activity are stored in a container, labeled, and located near the appropriate zone. Anyone can walk into the space and see how it functions.

Plan work zones. The prolific author, poet, and playwright Sir Walter Scott had a large desk with two working surfaces making it possible for him to work on multiple projects at once. I've adopted Scott's practice and added a second desk in my office. I use that desk to work on projects that don't require a computer. When we physically shift spaces, we remind our brain that it's time to switch activities. Think about how you can make use of various spaces in your office to more easily shift between work activities.

Move furniture, technology, and tools into the optimum positions. Consider where you want your desk—do you want to be able to look out the window or face the door? What kind of desk placement will help you access outlets, wall space, and light?

Create project shelves, bins, or bags. Your office might not be big enough to have separate zones for each work project. But you can set up a project shelf, bin, or bag. Collect all of your materials for each project and place them together. Label them clearly.

Group like elements together. For example, you might set aside a bin in your closet for office supplies or a shelf for writing books.

Create a clean working surface. Keep one area of your desk clear and free of clutter so that you can work.

Step Three: Try It Out!

Try writing in this newly zoned office. As before, keep track of what works and what challenges you. And, if the zones don't work the first time—rearrange your office. It often takes more than one try to find the setup that works for you.

Game Play Tips

- Use Pinterest to collect images of offices, studios, and work spaces that inspire you.
- Try online sales forums, second hand stores, and rummage sales to furnish your office space. But don't skimp on your desk and chair—find products that support your back and neck so that you can work without pain.
- Do a minor clean up weekly. This will help you reset your zones and start fresh each week.
- Think about completing this entire quest at least once a year. It's especially helpful to rearrange things before a new project or when work priorities shift.
- Consider adding your digital information to this quest. What digital clutter gets in the way of completing your work? Create a system for tossing, moving, and categorizing your digital clutter.

For the Win

When we organize our space, we demonstrate that we're professionals who deserve to work in a clean, well-lit space. This practice will help us take ourselves and our work more seriously.

35. JOURNAL TO BOOST PRODUCTIVITY

Exercise the writing muscle every day, even if it is only a letter, notes, a title list, a character sketch, a journal entry. Writers are like dancers, like athletes. Without that exercise, the muscles seize up.

– Jane Yolen

Many great writers kept diaries, including Franz Kafka, Sylvia Plath, and David Sedaris. Virginia Woolf was an avid diarist and wrote regularly about her family, literary gatherings, and her own writing. In one entry she wrote this about the habit of writing:

> But what is more to the point is my belief that the habit of writing thus for my own eye only is good practice. It loosens the ligaments. Never mind the misses and the stumbles. Going at such a pace as I do I must make the most direct and instant shots at my object, and thus have to lay hands on words, choose them and shoot them with no more pause than is needed to put my pen in the ink. I believe that during the past year I can trace some increase of ease in my professional writing which I attribute to my casual half hours after tea.[35]

A woman I know decided to get organized and used a journal to do it. She wrote down everything in a single journal: phone messages, to-do lists, meeting notes, ideas, and more. I liked the idea. As someone who has journals for just about every single thing I do—the project journal, the blog journal, the daily journal, the dream journal—this sounded doable. I've started carrying my regular journal with me. I tend to use it for every-thing: taking notes at author events and business conversations, recording random ideas and bits of dialogue, working through pitches and more.

Journaling can boost writing productivity in multiple ways. In this quest, you will explore several ways to journal and assess what works best for you.

The Quest

Choose one of the following journaling tools and try it for several sessions. Reflect on how it impacts your attitude, creativity, and productivity. If the first tool you use doesn't support your life, creative work, or writing, try another one.

Morning Pages or Evening Pages

Make your first or last action of the day a written one. Jot down one to three sloppy pages of anything that comes to your mind: words, images, memories, events, experiences, whatever. David Sedaris wrote, "I've been keeping a diary for 33 years and write in it every morning. Most of it's just whining, but every so often there'll be something I can use later: a joke, a description, a quote. It's an invaluable aid when it comes to winning arguments. 'That's not what you said on February 3, 1996,' I'll say to someone."[36]

Gratitude

For people who like more structure in their morning or evening pages, I suggest using the time to record their blessings. A gratitude journal can help the writer pay attention to the day. Once a day, record people or experiences that you feel thankful for. You might also make a game of it by setting up a gratitude scavenger hunt. In the morning, challenge yourself to look for three images of beauty, three acts of kindness, or even three different kinds of birds. You'll be surprised at how that small act of intention will help you see more to be grateful for.

Plan

Other quests in this book have encouraged you to write to plan. Research suggests that people who know the when, where, and what of their tasks tend to accomplish them. So if you've planned to write a blog post on composting tomorrow from 3-4 PM at your favorite indie coffee shop— and you write that down in your journal—you're much more likely to do it than, say, the person who thinks, *I'll do some sort of a blog post this week.* The plan doesn't have to be a technical "how I'm going to do it" document. If you're a creative, chances are that won't work for you. Try mind mapping, making a list, or drawing a map. Try journaling to plan: the next day, the next year, your new book, whatever.

The Bullet Journal

Ryder Carroll developed the Bullet Journal, an organized way to put everything you do in a single journal. Bullet Journals are usually paginated blank books that include several regular items: an index, a yearly log, a monthly log, weekly spreads, and daily entries. Many people who keep bullet journals also create collection pages for items that go together like books to read or movies to see. Project pages are also a popular feature in bullet journals and are used to plan work or personal projects, like a blog, a new book, or a vacation.

Try using your journal as a planning guide. Record to-do lists, ideas for your blog post, and anything else that might be helpful for your writing work. Tape or paste in information, inspiration, or photos. If you're using an electronic journal, you can simply take a picture and add it to your file.

Journal of a Book

For the past ten years, I've kept a journal for every single one of my books. I got the idea from Elizabeth George, who spoke about it when she visited my hometown for a book signing many years ago. She got the idea from John Steinbeck and wrote about it in her book on writing, *Write Away*:

> I've begun every day by writing in a journal, sometimes about the writing I'm doing, sometimes about what's on my mind at that moment. So for each novel I now write, I create a new journal entry, but before I do that, I read a day in the *last* Journal of a Novel for the previous novel. This allows me to see that, whatever I might be experiencing at the moment, I have experienced it and survived it before.[37]

Create a journal for your novel, nonfiction book, or blog in any way that works for you. It can also be a story bible or idea file, where you keep all the bits of information you need to tell the story.

Art Journaling

Any of the journal types above can be done as an art journal. Don't worry about how it looks. Explore and have fun. Here are some ideas for how to use an art journal.

- Explore an idea through art using any medium that feels fun to you including crayons, collage, doodling, or painting.
- Use art to record an experience or sighting, like attending a car show or watching squirrels dig up the seeds in your garden.
- Use your journal to explore color, texture, shape, and more.
- Try a visual writing form, such as found poetry (see "67. Exercise Writing Muscles" on page 205), collage poetry, or black out poetry.

Game Play Tips

- The list above provides a good start for journaling, but there are many other ways to use your journal. Try doing writing exercises, self-help exercises, or dream journaling.
- The tools presented in this quest overlap and most can be used in combination with each other.
- Choose the medium that works for you. Some people prefer to journal on paper, and most prefer a specific kind of journal. But

there are also several good journaling apps for phones and tablets that you might explore.

- Watch for perfectionism. Your journal should be a place where you can be messy and have fun. Don't worry about keeping it neat.

For the Win

Journaling can be a powerful tool for writers. Before tackling the crappy first draft, the journal allows us to think on paper without any worry about the outcome. Journaling practice strengthens our writing and helps us ignore the inner critic.

36. MOVE YOUR BODY

All truly great thoughts are conceived while walking.

– Friedrich Nietzsche

We're a sedentary culture. We sit to work and to relax. Studies suggest that the sedentary work life leads to obesity and heart disease. Eighty percent of today's jobs require little or no physical activity, up from 50 percent in 1960.[38] Because we sit at work, we're not burning the calories that people who have an active job burn through physical movement. Even regular exercisers who spend oodles of time sitting are at risk.

We need to change our habits. While we've got to put our butt in the chair to write our books, we must also get out of those chairs and move around more often. Many exercise experts suggest that we might get more benefit from our workouts if we spread them throughout the day. And here's the big bonus: regular movement and exercise throughout the day will increase your energy and help you connect to new ideas for your writing.

In this quest, you will consider multiple ways to stay active throughout the day. Choose a few and incorporate them into your daily routine until they become habits.

The Quest

When you tackle this quest, set a goal and then use your movement monitor to track your progress. When you hit your goal, give yourself a reward.

Know Your Baseline

Before you begin to add or increase your daily exercise, get a tool to monitor your activity level. Keep a record of your current daily movement level with an exercise tracker, like a Fitbit, or a smartphone app. Most exercise trackers record steps, movement per hour, heart rate, and more. Use the tracker to measure just how active or sedentary you are right now. Once you know your baseline, you can start to add movement to your day.

Establish Regular Exercise Sessions

Your regular exercise sessions form your fitness foundation. Plus, daily exercise gives you an energy boost that will support you throughout the day. Start moving more by adding a regular exercise routine to your week. Aim for 4-6 thirty-minute sessions throughout the week. Start slowly. Moving too fast, too soon can leave you sore and discouraged.

Add Movement!

Add one or more of the following movement breaks throughout the day.

Take strength building and stretching breaks. When I was taking physical therapy for my neck, my PT suggested taking breaks from the computer to do the exercises she assigned. Being a compliant patient, I did what she asked. Once an hour, I got up and did my neck and shoulder stretches. Here's the thing: not only did I feel better, my day went faster, and my writing improved. Make a list of 5-10 exercises you can do without breaking a sweat—leg lifts, the plank, maybe even downward dog. Set your timer and, when it rings, take a five-minute exercise break.

Do chores. Instead of sitting at your desk for hours, getting up only to use the restroom and visit the kitchen, move your weekend chores to the workweek. Keep a list of small, active chores that you need to accomplish. These tasks might be the regular stuff that you do every day or week anyway, like doing laundry, washing dishes, or watering the garden. Consider adding chores that are easy to do like vacuuming a room, dusting the bookshelves, or sweeping the porch. Get up once an hour to do one of these small chores. If you tend to get lost in your work, set a timer to remind yourself to get up and perhaps another one to prompt you to go back to your desk. If you don't work at home, get up every hour and walk around the office or up and down the stairs.

Stand up. Stand whenever you have the chance. Consider buying a standing desk so that you can read, write, and edit on your feet. Or, you might create a treadmill desk. Take a look at your daily work tasks and consider which ones you can do standing or walking. Then try it!

Get a new chair. A number of my writing friends swear by their balance ball chairs. Some of them sit on a regular old balance ball while they are at the desk. The balance ball requires sitters to use core muscles to maintain a healthy posture. I sit on my balance ball when I watch television at night. That way, I'm not just sitting there—I'm doing something!

Pace. When I was a teenager, my parents used to tell me, "Stand still!" I could not just sit and have a conversation. I also needed to wiggle, dance, and pace while talking. My children do the same thing. I've started to revisit this habit now that I am trying to move more. When I need to think about how to express a difficult concept, I pace around the house. I also pace during phone calls and conversations with my family.

Cultivate inefficiency. Yeah, in this multi-tasking world, inefficiency is counterintuitive. It can also help your health. When I sort mail at the dining room table, I get extra steps by walking a few pieces of mail at a time into the kitchen, where I place them in the recycling bin. Sometimes it takes six trips to eliminate the pile, but I've just taken more than 100 extra steps!

Do your errands on foot. We live in a pedestrian neighborhood, so I walk to the library, grocery store, bookstore, and pharmacy. If you aren't so lucky, drive to a pedestrian neighborhood or a shopping plaza and walk to all of the stores you need to go to. Or when you drive to a place with a big parking lot, like the grocery store or movie theater, try parking farther from the door.

Game Play Tips
- Check with your doctor before beginning any rigorous exercise program.
- As you establish a regular exercise routine, try different exercises until you find what works for you and your schedule. Some people prefer group exercise while others are committed to exercising alone. Doing your core chunk of exercise at the same time each day, like walking or biking, can help you make it a habit.
- A trainer or physical therapist can suggest exercises that work for any fitness level. One person I know lifted soup cans while in his wheelchair until he became strong enough to do more.

For the Win
You may be wondering how you are going to get anything done if you are always getting up to exercise or pace or load the dishwasher. Here's what I've found: I actually get more done when I exercise or do chores throughout the day. Yup. The breaks act as power-ups, refreshing us—so that we spend more of our work time actually working and less of it staring into space or playing on social media.

37. READ AS A WRITER

If you want to be a writer, you must do two things above all others: read a lot and write a lot. There's no way around these two things that I'm aware of, no shortcut.

– Stephen King

I have met many writers who do not read. That's like being a professional baseball player who loves to play baseball but refuses to watch the game. A good baseball player will learn and study the rules of the game, the statistics and quirks of each team and player, and the unique features of each stadium. In order to be successful in the book business, writers need to know and understand the playing field. The reading life provides the foundation for the writing life. If you want to write anything—nonfiction books, novels, blog posts, articles, or speeches—you need to develop a reading life.

Here's why:

- Reading good books will teach you how to write better. We learn by watching the masters do it well—whether it's baseball, cooking, or writing. Whenever you have a question about how to do something in your book, other books can be your models and teachers.
- Reading books in your field or genre will help you to create a book that can match or beat the competition. Writing a mediocre book won't help you or your business. When you read books, always ask yourself how yours can be better or different.
- Reading books in your field or genre, published by the best publishers, will teach you what the market wants. Pay attention to what sells—that tells you what readers are looking for.

This quest will help you develop a reading plan and follow it.

The Quest
You will create a wish list of books and other reading material that jazzes you, collect some of these items, create a reading schedule, and read. Wow! Because this quest contains so many steps, give yourself enough time to complete it.

Step One: Create a Reading Wish List

List your interests. What are you curious about? Before you begin to look for reading material, list everything you are interested in learning more about. Are there fields of study that intrigue you? What kinds of ideas inspire you? Are there locations or life situations that you've always wanted to know more about?

Consider:

Read anything that you experience as delicious or fun or engaging. What do you remember enjoying reading as a child or in the past? When I was in graduate school studying theology, I often read fiction in between theological tomes. Once, I carried around Fath*er Melancholy's Daughter by* Gail Godwin. My classmates teased me for reading "trash" when I should have been reading God's Word. (Perhaps they'd never found the truth about God in fiction.) The same or worse may happen to you when you pick up a kid's book, graphic novel, erotic fiction, or ancient Greek literature. Put your own book cover around it and read it anyway.

Read the books you wish you'd written. If you desire to write a specific kind of book—children's fiction, young adult, romance, business—then read everything you can get your hands on in the genre. Read the bestsellers, the best reviewed, and the best loved. Talk to your potential audience and ask them what they like to read—and read that.

Read what's popular in your field. Most professions have books, blogs, and periodicals that they consider standard reading material. Review professional development sites, popular books and blogs, and other news sites for reading recommendations.

Read what your competition is writing. If you hope to be a famous romance novelist or mystery writer, it helps to read what other writers are publishing. Speakers and business owners who write books might read the books that their competitors and colleagues are writing. It's helpful to read the books critics consider good, what the readers are buying, and what excites you.

Step Two: Gather Reading Material!

Once you have a list of ideas and subjects you are curious about, you can begin to gather your reading material. Consider what you would like to read in these areas:

Newspapers. Find a newspaper that you like, and subscribe to it. Or, subscribe to it online and make it your homepage or bookmark it.

Online newsletters. I try to subscribe to a number of newsletters, press release services, and list serves in my areas of interest. This provides me with great new information on a regular basis.

Blogs. Blogs are an amazing source of information and tools. Use a blog reading tool to make reading easier.

Periodicals. The library is a great source for reviewing magazines before you commit to a subscription. When you get stuck for ideas or need a brain treat, purchase an interesting magazine for your weekly reading time.

Podcasts. Some of the best content today is being broadcast as podcasts. Like the first-rate radio, podcasts exist in almost every genre and can entertain, terrify, and educate the listener. Try out a few online and then subscribe to your favorites.

Books. All of the above resources are a great source of information for great books to read. If you need more ideas, talk to a bookseller, librarian, or writer. Don't forget to consider books in all formats: paper, digital, and audio.

Step Three: Get Access!

Ever have one of those moments when you have nothing to read? It drives me crazy to be stuck somewhere without the gentle distraction of words. In order to make reading a habit or simply to save your sanity, always have reading material accessible.

- Keep a book or magazine with you at all times. If possible, put a digital reading platform on your smart phone or iPad or carry a digital reading device, so that you can read even when you forget to take that book with you!
- Keep an audio book and several podcasts on your smart phone so you can listen while running, driving, cleaning the house, crafting, cooking dinner, and more.
- Always keep a stack of books and periodicals in the bathroom.
- Keep a book in the car (or on your person) for the times you end up waiting.

- Keep a book in the kitchen so you can read while you wait for the water to boil or coffee to brew.

Step Four: Schedule Time to Read

Even though I have managed to make reading a priority for 20 years, I still need to schedule time to read. This year, I am planning on adding a reading afternoon to my weekly schedule to keep up with the big shelf of books I want to read (not to mention the magazines, ezines, blogs, and other material).

Here are some ways to add a few minutes of reading to your day. And remember, any of these options can be done with any kind of material—a physical book or magazine, an e-reader, or an audio book :

- Get up 30 minutes earlier than your family and use the time for a quiet breakfast and reading.
- Read or listen to an audio book while you exercise.
- Commute to work and read or listen to a book on the bus or train.
- Listen to an audio book while you drive.
- Listen to audio books while you clean, craft, or do other household tasks.
- Read during your lunch hour.
- Take a reading break.
- Set aside 30 minutes at the end of the workday to catch up on blog reading or other online reading before you turn off the computer for the day.
- Set aside work time each week to catch up on the reading you do for your profession.
- Replace one hour of email or computer time with reading.
- DVR all television shows—and get back 20 minutes per hour show to read!
- Stop watching television a little earlier (or start watching a little later), and take back an hour or more for reading.
- Set aside time every weekend to read.
- Dedicate one afternoon (or day) per week (or month) as a reading retreat—and head out to a coffee shop, park, or library to read.

Step Five: Read

Put the plan into practice and read. Review your progress after a week or two, and make revisions as necessary.

Game Play Tips

- Consider doing this quest on a free day or weekend as a reading retreat.
- Keep sticky notes, a journal, or other recording device near you so you can note passages you want to reflect on, review later, or refer to in your own work.
- Note the books you want to read and keep track of the books you've read on a site like Goodreads or LibraryThing. If you're reading in your field, consider publishing lists or reviews of your favorite reads on social media or your blog.

For the Win

Reading is a habit that takes time to establish—like exercising and eating well. My final bit of advice will help you ease into it: start with a book that rocks your world. Don't try to devour *War and Peace* if you haven't read anything since college. You'll just get frustrated. Instead, pick up a book that helps you lose track of time. You'll get hooked. I promise!

PART THREE: MASTER YOUR MINDSET

38. Examine Your Thoughts
Examine the negative chatter and unhelpful stories that dominate your thoughts.

39. Blast Those Obstacles
Use "if-then" statements to overcome obstacles.

40. Lasso of Truth
Identify limiting beliefs and use the lasso of truth to dismiss them.

41. Adopt a Positive Mantra
Create and use a positive statement to interrupt negative thoughts.

42. Drop Everything and Write
Let go of worries, fears, and complaints to write.

43. Overcome Fear to Write Now
Eliminate fear by facing it.

44. Master Your Mornings
Create a morning ritual that supports your creativity.

45. Define Your Purpose
Use your purpose as a tool to overcome fear and negativity.

46. Innovate and Boost Creativity
Try a new experience to spark creativity.

47. Reframe Blocks
Reimagine new solutions for a problem.

48. Overcome Perfectionism
Use intentions to ditch perfectionism and write.

49. Explain Well
Learn the most helpful way to explain difficult experiences.

38. EXAMINE YOUR THOUGHTS

If you are not afraid of the voices inside you, you will not fear the critics outside you.

– Natalie Goldberg

What's in your brain?

In John Green's novel, *Turtles All The Way Down*, sixteen-year-old Aza Holmes suffers from Obsessive Compulsive Disorder (OCD). She's plagued by negative thoughts that spiral out of control at times. She says, "The thing about a spiral is, if you follow it inward, it never actually ends. It just keeps tightening, infinitely."[39]

Aza is not alone. Many people are plagued by repetitive negative thoughts. Some suffer from OCD, anxiety, depression, or another mental health issue. But others simply can't let go of the challenging things that people have said to them or the things that have happened to them. Psychology researchers write about the negativity bias or the negativity effect—the tendency of humans to listen to, learn from, and use negative experiences more frequently than positive ones.[40]

These negative thoughts and stories impact our life, creative endeavors, and writing. When we are unable to focus or the writing doesn't go well, we might think: *I don't have the kind of focus it takes to write* or *I'm not smart enough* or *I don't have talent*.

When I have a difficult week with writing or life, my coach asks me, "What are you telling yourself?" In this quest, you'll examine the negative chatter and unhelpful stories that dominate your thoughts.

The Quest

In meditation practice, we notice our thoughts and then let them go. In this quest, you will notice the thoughts and stories that emerge during your working day, leisure time, and writing sessions and record them.

Step One: Record Recurring Thoughts

Do you already know the negative thoughts and stories that plague you? Most of us are pretty aware of what we tell ourselves—after all, we've lived with these stories for years. Take 20-30 minutes to record the messages you tell yourself regularly.

Step Two: Record Intrusive Thoughts

For the next week, keep a notebook or phone near you while you work and record any intrusive or negative thoughts that show up. If you have a list of negative thoughts and stories from step one, it may be helpful to print it out and carry it with you. Then you can place a check mark by any thoughts that appear. If it's difficult to stop and note thoughts as they occur, simply record negative thoughts at the end of each day.

Step Three: Compile a List

Once you've examined your thoughts and stories for a week or so, compile a list of the messages that repeatedly appear. Make a special note of any thoughts that stall your writing or other creative work. Hold onto this list. This will be a helpful resource in the next quests.

Game Play Tips

- Pay special attention to the thoughts and stories that feel very old—messages you received as a child or young adult. These may be more ingrained in your psyche than other ideas and might hold the feeling of truth.
- After doing this quest, you might feel discouraged or down, and no wonder: you've just spent the week listening to your negative inner voices. Nurture yourself. Say kind things, take a fun outing, or indulge in a treat like a massage.
- In addition to practicing extreme self-care, practice some of the power-ups (see "Power-up List" on page 237) listed in the Appendix.

For the Win

I have a particularly loud and nasty inner critic who shows up frequently to chastise me for my sins, large and small. When I forget small things, like making the bed or saying thank you, she screams at me as if I've committed a mortal sin. A friend frequently asks me: "Don't you ever talk back to her?" In the next quests, you'll learn how to manage this inner critic and add some positive inner voices as well.

39. BLAST THOSE OBSTACLES

Obstacles don't have to stop you. If you run into a wall, don't turn around and give up. Figure out how to climb it, go through it, or work around it.

– Michael Jordan

What thoughts, feelings, or practices interrupt your creative work?

When I was finishing my first graduate degree, I was awarded a fellowship for a second Master's Degree. I'd receive tuition, food, and housing for a year. In exchange, I was expected to teach, take classes, and write a thesis. The dean expressed her doubts about my potential for success: "You're all over the place. You have too many ideas and no focus. I can't imagine you finishing this degree."

Though the dean predicted my failure, I succeeded. At the end of the year, I graduated—with distinction. Despite my success, her words haunt me to this day. When I'm struggling to finish projects, I still hear her voice saying, "You'll never finish, you have too many ideas and no focus."

That's when I need to get out my secret weapon: the Obstacle Blaster.

Over the years, I've faced many obstacles to writing success. Some of them have been external: Sick children. Time constraints. Tight markets. Most have been internal: Fear, frustration, doubt, and overwhelm. The Obstacle Blaster helps with both external and internal obstacles.

Psychologist Peter Gollwitzer discovered that children who could imagine not only possible obstacles but also how to overcome them were more able to accomplish their goals.[41] The successful children followed their worried "what ifs" with concrete ideas about how they might handle any obstacle. Gollitzer calls this "implementation intention" or an "if-then plan." I call it the Obstacle Blaster. In this quest, you will develop your own Obstacle Blaster.

The Quest

If you haven't done the previous quest, "38. Examine Your Thoughts" on page 128, list your fears and any other thought that has become an obstacle for you. They might look something like this:

What if I have too many ideas and don't finish my article on time?

I'm overwhelmed, what if I can't figure out how to write this book?

I'm frustrated, my kids are sick again. What if I can't finish my work?

Brainstorm Solutions
Choose one obstacle and brainstorm ways to solve it.

Obstacle: What if I have too many ideas and don't finish my article on time?

Possible solutions: Write down all ideas. Think about how to use all of them. Think about how to use just one of them. Talk through the article with a friend. Set aside time to work on just the article. List topics to cover in the article and work on them one at a time.

Write Statements
Write one or more "if-then" statements to help you overcome the obstacle. Here's mine:

> **If** *I feel overwhelmed and have trouble focusing,* **then** *I will list the topics I want to cover in the article and work on them one at a time.*

See how easy that is?

Game Play Tips
- The Obstacle Blaster works brilliantly on many kinds of obstacles. If you have difficulty using it to overcome writing or creative obstacles, try it on something more concrete—like overcoming obstacles to get to the gym.
- When you write your if-then intention, make sure that your promise is something within your control. External events like sick kids, work deadlines, and noisy neighbors might not respond to the Obstacle Blaster. That's okay—change the things you can change. You'll still move forward.
- If you get stuck and cannot dream up solutions, call on your allies (see "26. Identify Your Allies" on page 91) to brainstorm with you. It's amazing how other people can see solutions when we see only blocks!

For the Win
Now that you have the Obstacle Blaster, you can take on the concrete challenges and limiting beliefs that you've been hanging onto for too long. Blast them and let them go!

40. LASSO OF TRUTH

What in fact I keep choosing
are these words, these whispers, conversations
from which time after time the truth breaks moist and green.

– Adrienne Rich

One spring, I taught writing to middle school students. When I read to them or demonstrated the assignment, I heard a lot of groans and a few bad words. But nothing compared to the complaining that happened when it was their turn to write. Some students said, "I don't understand this." Or "I can't write. Ask my teacher." Others blamed me, "Why're you making us do this? Why can't we paint?" And a few just put their heads down and slept.

After many weeks of struggling to get the students interested enough to participate, I stepped back and observed. I asked questions. I realized that my students were struggling with limiting beliefs or ideas that were holding them back. In order to move forward, they needed to tackle those limiting beliefs and discover new ways of thinking about themselves.

Limiting beliefs can be held about oneself, other people, groups, or the world.[42] They often sound like this:

- I do/I don't... (*I'm a nonfiction writer. I don't do fiction.*)
- I can't... (*I can't dance. I can't write dialogue. I can't speak in public.*)
- I must/mustn't or should/shouldn't... (*I should clean the house before writing. I shouldn't write fiction until I've taken more classes.*)
- I am/am not... (*I'm not good enough.*)
- I want, but... (*I want to write, but I'm feeling overwhelmed.*)
- I would, but... (*I would write, but I need more training.*)
- I tried, but... (*I tried to get published, but it's too hard.*)

We're all susceptible to limiting beliefs. Some of us have a constant stream of negative thoughts running through our heads. And even if we don't, we run into friends and family members who're happy to remind us of our limits. Here are a few limiting beliefs I've heard:

- *You write nonfiction. How can you write a novel without going to school?*
- *Shouldn't you get a real job?*
- *I don't know how you can leave your children to go to a writing conference.*

When limiting beliefs threaten to interrupt or stop our writing, we need help—and fast. And I've got it: Wonder Woman's Lasso of Truth. In this quest, you'll learn how to use the Lasso of Truth to dump your limiting beliefs.

The Quest

Wonder Woman used the Lasso of Truth to trap her enemies and force them to tell the truth. You can use this tool to find the truth behind the lies you tell yourself about writing.

Step One: Name the Obstacles

Use the list you created in "38. Examine Your Thoughts" on page 128 or observe your thoughts and make a list of the ones that have become obstacles for you. These are the ideas that keep you from achieving your goals—writing the book, sending off the query, telling the truth about your life. Examples might be:

- *I'm not a good enough writer to get published.*
- *I'm too busy to write.*
- *Nobody thinks I'm disciplined enough to write a book.*

If there are additional limiting beliefs that support these thoughts, record those, too. So, let's say your limiting thought is, *I'm not disciplined enough to write a book.* Behind the thought might be beliefs like, *I can't stick to an exercise program, how can I write a book?* or *I've never written anything that long.* or *I would try, but I'm pretty sure I'd fail.*

Step Two: Lasso and Question!

You now have a big list of limiting thoughts and beliefs that you can challenge. Take out your Lasso of Truth and question those thoughts. Yup, that's right. Don't let those beliefs sit there, looking all smug on the page. Challenge them.

Byron Katie is known for challenging the stories that limit us. Use her questions[43] to challenge your beliefs:

- Is that true?
- Can you absolutely know it's true?
- How do you react or what happens when you believe that thought?
- Who would you be without that thought?

Step Three: Turn Around

Once you've run through the list of questions for the thoughts, try turning the thought around. According to Katie, there are three ways to turn around thoughts: to the self, the other, and the opposite.[44] So the belief, *I'm too busy to write! My family and friends need me.* might become:

- To the self: *I have plenty of time to write.*
- To the other: *I need my friends and family. My friends and family need me to write.*
- To the opposite: *I have enough time. My friends and family will support my writing.*

Whoa!

After years of telling yourself, *I'm too busy to write*, the opposite idea might seem ludicrous. And no wonder: the negative thought is embedded in your brain. But it doesn't have to be that way.

Here's when we really need the Lasso of Truth. Sit with the new idea for just a minute. Then, look at your life for evidence of the new truth. If your new truth is, *I have enough time. My friends and family will support my writing*, list any example of how you have enough time and how others support your writing, no matter how small.

Once you have a list, review each item on the list and then repeat the reversed thought. Try to feel the truth of the new thought in your body. Know with your whole being that this new idea is true.

Once you have completed this process, jot your positive statements on an index card and keep them near you.

Game Play Tips

- Limiting beliefs are often deeply ingrained. We develop many of them as children and young adults, and it's difficult to just let them go after one or two sessions of challenging them. Commit to working on this quest repeatedly until you are able to recognize and challenge the limiting beliefs.
- Because limiting beliefs are deeply rooted and habitual, they will continue to show up as negative inner thoughts or messages from our inner critic. As you are working to change them with the lasso of truth and adopt new, more expansive beliefs, you may need to act "as if" you believe them. That's what the students I mentioned above did—and it made it possible for them to write.
- Limiting beliefs can be sneaky! While we're working on eliminating them from our writing life, they may pop up in our work, personal, or family life. Just notice this—and gently shift the messages to healthier, more positive ways of thinking.

- The positive statements you create while doing this quest can become the mantras that you repeat to yourself as you work to renew your mindset. You'll create and use more mantras in "41. Adopt a Positive Mantra" on page 136.

For the Win

Once you've taken those limiting beliefs, questioned them and reversed them, it's time to get writing. Don't let the obstacles hold you back from achieving your dream! You got this!

41. ADOPT A POSITIVE MANTRA

Always remember, your focus determines your reality.

– George Lucas

Have you noticed the pop-up trend online? Many websites feature pop-up windows that invite the user to sign up for a newsletter or a coupon. Other online stores use pop-up windows that offer to "Live Chat" with site visitors. And recently when I check some of my favorite online sites from my phone, a page regularly opens and tells me, "Congratulations, you may have won an iPhone." When I click on the back button, the page reloads. The only way out is to type the URL of the page I want in the address bar. And even then, the ad often pops up again within minutes.

This pop-up phenomenon reminds me of my brain. When I'm writing, taking care of my family, or taking a walk, negative thoughts pop up and distract me. More often than not, these thoughts aren't helpful—they're negative, persistent, and distracting. I'm not alone. Many of my clients and colleagues report the same phenomenon—negative messages assailing them especially when they are focused on important work.

In Tibetan Buddhism, practitioners use a mind-training tool called Lojong or slogan practice to extend compassion to themselves, others, and the world throughout the day. Lojong includes 59 slogans on a variety of themes. According to Buddhist nun Pema Chodron, Lojong practice helps us see the challenging aspects of life as opportunities to awaken our compassion. Throughout the day, the practitioner focuses on a single mantra to help them let go of disturbing thoughts and focus on more generative beliefs. Once a slogan becomes rooted in our belief system, the practitioner moves onto the next one.[45]

In *Habit Changers: 82 Game-Changing Mantras to Mindfully Realize Your Goals*, author and executive coach M. J. Ryan introduces mantras that help the modern reader adapt this practice to address common negative patterns. According to Ryan, our brains conserve energy by adopting "habits of thinking and acting."[46] These habits drive our behavior. Ryan created each of the one-liners to help readers override the automatic thoughts and habits and act purposefully.

As writers, our negative thinking patterns often interrupt or halt our writing practice. We learned that in the previous quest, "40. Lasso of Truth" on page 132. The inner critic attacks us with negative beliefs:

- *No one will buy this story.*
- *I'll never finish this project.*
- *I don't know enough to write this.*

Lojong practice or habit changers can help us replace these negative thoughts a little bit at a time. I've appreciated the mantras Rose created for her book. Now when I feel worried that I haven't accomplished enough, I repeat the mantra, "You are where you're supposed to be." When I compare myself to other writers, I say, "Walk your own path." And when I have trouble knowing what to choose or how to spend my time, I say, "Trust your inner GPS."

In this quest, you will choose one negative persistent thought and create a new mantra to replace it.

The Quest

In see "40. Lasso of Truth" on page 132, you challenged limiting beliefs. In this quest, you'll take a negative thought—possibly one you worked with in "Lasso of Truth"—and create a one-line mantra to replace it with. You can use the information you gathered from "38. Examine Your Thoughts" on page 128 or "Lasso of Truth" to help you identify negative thoughts.

Step One: Choose a Thought

Choose the negative thought that bothers you most right now, possibly one that surfaces repeatedly.

Step Two: Create a Mantra

Create a one-line mantra that you can use to replace this thought. Here are some examples:

- Instead of *No one will buy this story*, try *I trust that the right editor is waiting to read my story* or *I trust that this story will find a home*.
- Instead of *I'll never finish this project*, try *One step at a time*.
- Instead of *I don't know enough to write this*, try *I know just enough to write the next part*.

Step Three: Repeat the Mantra

Repeat the phrase at set times throughout the day, especially when the negative thought appears. You might tie this mantra to your creative process, and repeat it before and after your writing session.

Game Play Tips

- Write your positive mantra on an index card or large piece of paper and post it where you can see it.
- Create a graphic with your mantra on it and use it on your computer, phone, or tablet.
- Choose a cue to remind yourself to repeat the mantra. Tie it to an activity, like going online, or to an external event, like the phone ringing.

  When you have mastered one mantra, choose a new one.

For the Win

This practice may seem simple—and it is. That's why it works. It helps us retrain our brain one small step at a time.

42. DROP EVERYTHING AND WRITE

We are the stories we live! The tales we tell ourselves!
— Clay Kaczmarek, *Assassin's Creed Brotherhood*

For many of us, our work is not just our work, it's who we are. We write as an extension of our lives. As we give voice to characters or explain how things work, we are figuring out our own worlds. Because of this, our emotions can interact with our work. Sometimes this is helpful—it brings depth to our writing. But sometimes these emotions get in the way of doing our best work.

In the book, *Organize Your Mind, Organize Your Life: Train Your Brain to Get More Done in Less Time* by Paul Hammerness, M.D., Margaret Moore, and John Hane, the authors identify three unhelpful emotions that we often bring to our work: anxiety, sadness, and anger.[47] We worry about being good enough, we worry that other writers are doing better, we get sad when our work is overlooked, we get angry at those who don't respect us, and on it goes. Who can write with that kind of junk in our heads?

When my daughter was in grade school and middle school, they had DEAR time every single day—drop everything and read. In her school, not having a DEAR book was an offense punishable with detention.

When I think about DEAR time, I wonder: what if the "everything" we have to drop is our worry, complaining, and negative self talk?

In the book, *Organize Your Mind, Organize Your Life*, the authors refer to the swirling thoughts and emotions in our brains as *frenzy*. We can tame the frenzy by engaging the prefrontal cortex of the brain. This can be challenging to do when our inner critic is having a hissy fit. This quest will help you drop your worries, complaints, and fears and write.

The Quest

Next time you're writing, and the inner critic showers you with doubts, pause. When you're tempted to whine instead of write, catch yourself. Gently tell yourself to stop, saying, *I commit to drop everything and write.* Then recite one of your mantras—from "40. Lasso of Truth" on page 132 or "41. Adopt a Positive Mantra" on page 136—and write. If gentle doesn't work, just shout: *Drop the story!* or even, *Plot twist!* And write!

I can guarantee you that the negative critic or the urge to complain will hit you again, very quickly and even harder. Repeat the implementation process: gently tell the inner critic to stop talking, recite the mantra, and write. Tweak this as needed. You might take a walk around the block or do a yoga pose to help yourself let go of the negative thoughts and grab onto the positive ones.

Game Play Tips

- When the frenzy is strong, repeating a mantra may not be enough to ease the anxiety. In those times, it can be helpful to engage the prefrontal cortex. Try reading a complex text or playing a game like Sudoku. Once you activate your prefrontal cortex, the frenzy will slow down.
- In my child's school, DEAR time was always scheduled. For those who write only when inspired, negative self-talk and complaining get in the way of even getting to the writing. Boost your chances of making this quest work by scheduling time to write. For help with scheduling, check out "19. Detect Your Genius Time" on page 72, "28. Develop a Writing Habit" on page 97, and "31. Cluster Tasks" on page 104.
- I often think my affirmations sound too much like Stuart Smalley's script from *Saturday Night Live*, and I can't stop laughing. If affirmations trigger laughter or cringing, play around with them until you discover a few that work.

For the Win

We can become addicted to our negative stories about ourselves. Sometimes it feels easier to cling to our regrets, rehash our failures, or repeat our negative beliefs. But we can also find healing through writing. Commit to dropping the negative voices and stories that interrupt your creative process and write!

43. OVERCOME FEAR TO WRITE NOW

What she said was:
Dear Otto,
We're all scared, most of the time. Life would be lifeless if we weren't.
Be scared, and then jump into that fear. Again and again. Just
remember to hold onto yourself while you do it.
Sincerely, Etta

– Emma Hooper

What's keeping you from writing your book?

My clients hire me because they have a deep desire to write a book but they've bumped into an obstacle that keeps them from writing. Here's what clients tell me about the blocks they face:

- *I'm stuck. I don't know where or how to start.*
- *I struggle with procrastination.*
- *I can't seem to find the time to write.*
- *Every time I try to write, my ADHD kicks in. I get monkey mind and can't focus.*
- *I get so overwhelmed by the process.*
- *I've started several books, but I can't seem to finish them.*
- *I wonder if I'm too old.*
- *I've got so much research to do before I can start.*

This book is packed full of tools to overcome every one of these challenges. But when the tools don't work, I know that these blocks are simply hiding a deeper issue: fear.

Wait! Wouldn't fear feel like we're facing down a dangerous beast? Wouldn't we have a racing heart, sweaty palms, and a flopping stomach?

Sometimes. But fear can be sneaky, and it often masquerades as:

- Perfectionism (*I have to make this piece perfect before I can share it.*)
- Excuses (*I'm too tired to write.*)
- Procrastination (*Before I can write, I need to clean the house, take a class, finish this research.*)

Though each of us experiences fear in different ways, we all get the same result: we don't write. Or, if we write, we don't share our work. We hide behind excuses and blocks.

So how do you know if your obstacle or writer's block is really fear? If you have reviewed and revised your external challenges to writing (e.g., found a time and place to write), tried some of the quests in this book geared to help you manage your mindset, and worked through the tools designed to help you overcome the most common obstacles people face (see "Part Five: Overcome Obstacles" on page 189) and still cannot write, chances are you're dealing with fear.

Here's the thing: if our core issue is fear, then strategies are less likely to work. We can have the best software, the perfect schedule, and an ideal outline—and we'll still procrastinate. Why? Because fear hurts. It feels uncomfortable, and we'll do whatever we can to avoid feeling it.

When we went to Disney World, my family challenged me to go on a roller coaster. They chose a small one at Animal Kingdom, one that was suitable for ages 3 and up. I climbed into the ride, making sure my safety belt was tightly fastened. And then I reassured myself: you can do anything for a few minutes. The ride started out fast and never let up. I screamed and swore because, dang, the twists and drops had left my stomach and my courage back at the starting gate. But it was over fast.

It's the same with any emotion: they pass through us quite quickly—in about 90 seconds. I first heard about the 90-second rule in a class with Martha Beck. She said that most feelings take just 90 seconds to run through our bodies.

Jill Bolte Taylor talks about this in her book, *My Stroke of Insight*:

> Once triggered, the chemical released by my brain surges through my body and I have a physiological experience. Within 90 seconds from the initial trigger, the chemical component of my anger has completely dissipated from my blood and my automatic response is over. If, however, I remain angry after those 90 seconds have passed, then it is because I have chosen to let that circuit continue to run.[48]

This quest gives you a single tool for overcoming fear. But first a warning: you'll have to face your fear before you let it go. And some reassurance: it'll be over soon, and then you'll feel better.

The Quest

Next time you show up to write and feel fear—don't avoid it. Feel it. Ride it out for 90 seconds and then get back to writing. If you experience one of the roadblocks above—perfectionism, procrastination, or excuses—and suspect it's fear, try writing. If it's fear, it'll roar louder. Let it. Feel what's happening.

Feeling fear is tough. Trust me, I know. I've dealt with it my whole life. I'll do whatever I can to avoid it. It's uncomfortable, distressing, and just plain yucky.

Still, if you can take a deep breath and feel the fear, it will go away more quickly. Know this: you don't have to white knuckle it. Feel the fear with some kindness toward yourself. Talk to your anxious inner child the way you'd talk to any child who was afraid.

- *You are safe.*
- *You are okay.*
- *This feeling will pass.*
- *It will be fine.*

Once the fear has passed, get back to work.
Repeat this quest as often as necessary.

Game Play Tips

- Use any power-ups that will help you ride out the fear. I've given you one—speaking to yourself with comforting words. Others might include walking in nature, using affirmations, talking to a friend, and deep breathing. Try these out! They'll help.
- Fear often feels like someone has literally removed the ground beneath our feet. We feel like we're falling, arms flailing, with no safe place to go. Getting grounded can help counter this feeling. Take off your shoes and let your feet feel the ground. Imagine yourself growing roots into the earth. Other grounding exercises include hugging a tree (I'm not kidding!), wrapping four fingers around our thumbs on both hands and holding this hand position while breathing deeply, holding a comforting object like a stone or stuffed animal, or noticing concrete sensory details about your surroundings.
- Fear tends to show up when we're doing something new, working on a project that means a lot to us, or writing about something that's very personal. That's normal. So if the fear appears, acknowledge it, feel it, and keep writing.

For the Win

Most of the people who've accomplished great things or written amazing books have experienced and overcome fear. You are not alone. And you are not stuck. You can overcome the fear and write.

44. MASTER YOUR MORNINGS

No matter how dark the night, morning always comes, and our journey begins anew.

– Lulu, *Final Fantasy X*

Productivity experts talk about the value of morning routines to set up our days for success. For the past few years, I've been using a morning routine recommended by Tony Robbins.

Each morning, I take a 30-minute walk. I devote the first ten minutes to expressing gratitude for the gifts in my life. For the second ten minutes, I vision what I will accomplish during the day, sometimes even planning the small chunk I will be writing that morning. Finally, I spend the last ten minutes practicing what Tony Robbins calls "incantation" or saying positive mantras that help me experience what it will feel like to have accomplished my vision.

At first, I felt awkward working through this routine on my morning walks. But it sure beat my regular habit of obsessing over past mistakes and worrying about the future. After a time, the morning routine became a habit, and I miss it when I am unable to do it.

In this quest, you'll create your own morning mindset routine and practice it for several weeks.

The Quest

Morning mindset routines can help us reset our mindset, increase our feelings of well-being, and get stuff done. In this quest, you will choose from helpful mindset tools and design the ritual that works best for you.

Practices to Avoid

Most mindset writers agree that when we do any of the following practices first thing in the morning, it can create a negative mindset or trigger monkey mind: watching or listening to news, checking email, surfing social media, and texting.

Practices to Include

The following tools are often part of a healthy morning routine. Choose 2-5 of the following ingredients and play with combining them in an order that works for you. When you find the magic combination, practice it for a week or two and see how it affects your writing.

- Essential oils
- Exercise (walking, running, yoga, light stretching)
- Gratitude (verbal or written)
- Healthy food
- Journaling (morning pages; gratitude; day, week, or life planning; mantras)
- Meditation
- Prayer (written or verbal, traditional prayers or mantras)
- Reading (spiritual essays, artistic essays, poetry, personal development, or other affirming literature)
- Water

Game Play Tips

- Play with the practices. Try different practices, vary the order you do them in, or how you complete them. Even small tweaks can make a big difference.
- Combine well. I can't sit still in the morning, so combining my morning meditation ritual with walking has helped me focus. Consider how you can combine healthy rituals to get more out of your morning routine.
- Give these practices time to work. It often takes 2-3 weeks before a routine can feel, well, routine! And it takes 66 days for that routine to become a habit. But stick with it, because it's in the midst of nourishing routines that we often get our "aha!" moments.
- Change your routine with the season, event, or project. Different circumstances may require different routines. It can be helpful to have routines for unique circumstances—such as a change of season, holidays, big projects, or being stuck inside with a virus.

For the Win

Our mindset can make a huge difference in how we approach and appreciate life. When we transform a small part of our day, we ignite a process that can transform our entire day.

45. DEFINE YOUR PURPOSE

When I dare to be powerful, to use my strength in the service of my vision, then it becomes less and less important whether I am afraid.

– Audre Lorde

Negative voices emerge when we get disconnected from why we are writing, making art, launching a business, or doing any other hard thing. Positive messages help, but it can be difficult to overcome the negative voices in our head by simply replacing them with positive messages. Connecting to our purpose becomes a more powerful practice.

Many years ago, I interviewed writer Jeffrey Gingold. He spoke about being on a big television show with his book, *Facing the Cognitive Challenges of MS*. I asked if it was scary. He said, "When you are doing something to help people, fear doesn't matter." His words helped me to see the reason I was writing—to help people overcome their own fears.

In this quest, you'll consider your purpose and use it as a tool to overcome fear and negativity.

The Quest

Consider your current project. Open your journal and write about why you are working on this particular project. Are you hoping to help people, encourage others, create joy, entertain, or something else? List everything that applies.

Create a Purpose Statement

Once you have a list, turn each "why" into a purpose statement. So, "entertain" might become, *I am writing this book to engage readers and invite them to laugh!* Or "help people" might be, *I am launching this home study program to help people overcome financial blocks and tap into prosperity.*

Use Your Words

Choose one or two purpose statements and find a way to incorporate them in your daily life.

- Repeat them as a part of your morning routine.
- Put them in your phone, on your computer, or near your working desk as reminders to live according to your purpose.
- Keep one copy with you at all times, so you can access it whenever fear shows up.

Game Play Tips

- Revise your purpose statement for each project.
- If you have difficulty writing your purpose statement, refer back to "10. Write Goals that Work" on page 45 and the goals you wrote for that quest.
- If your purpose statement doesn't work or feel right, then try again. Dig deeper until you land at your true purpose.
- If you get stuck figuring out the why, ask a friend to interview you. Sometimes you can discover your motives behind your actions in conversation with other people.

For the Win

When we get connected to our purpose, we overcome fear. I've noticed that many writers who fear big crowds will brave them because they know the deeper purpose: to connect in a meaningful way with their readers. Whatever your purpose is, let that be more important than your fear. Get connected to why you write, and you'll always be able to put words on paper.

46. INNOVATE AND BOOST CREATIVITY

If you want something new, you have to stop doing something old.
– Peter Drucker

In the Oprah and Deepak meditation experience called *Getting Unstuck: Creating a Limitless Life!*, Deepak Chopra said, "It has been estimated that for most people half the thoughts they have today are the same as the ones that they had yesterday."

Wow.

I wonder:

- How many of our daily thoughts are negative? (Some say up to 70 percent, but I had difficulty finding research to prove that number.)
- How do repetitive thoughts impact our creative life?
- How can we stimulate new thinking?

Creativity is connected to neuroplasticity—the brain's potential to reorganize itself, creating new neural pathways. According to an article by science writer Brent Crane in *The Atlantic*:

> Neural pathways are influenced by environment and habit, meaning they're also sensitive to change: New sounds, smells, language, tastes, sensations, and sights spark different synapses in the brain and may have the potential to revitalize the mind.[49]

New experiences stimulate our brain and help us connect ideas, information, and experiences. These new connections can radically affect our creative work. As Steve Jobs said, "Creativity is just connecting things. When you ask creative people how they did something, they feel a little guilty because they didn't really do it, they just saw something."[50]

And more good news: when we experience something new, our brain releases dopamine. When our brain releases dopamine, it increases our desire to explore new things and receive a reward. What a lovely cycle! And we can kick it into high gear by purposefully seeking new experiences.[51]

If you're feeling stuck—mired in repetitive thoughts and habits, not sure how to solve your current creative problem, or confused about how to move forward with your writing project—you might need a dose of newness! This quest will get you out of your comfort zone to experience new things.

The Quest

Here are four proven ways to stretch your brain and spark creativity. Use them as starting points and dream up activities that energize you. Choose one or more to try. Once you've played with the experience, reflect on how it impacted your life.

Learn a Craft

A recent study demonstrated that seniors who learned a new skill, like quilting or Photoshop, improved their cognitive function.[52] But the benefits don't stop there. Repetitive crafts, like crochet, can reduce stress as effectively as meditation. Plus, research shows that crafting can have a dopamine effect, improve our sense of self-efficacy, and reduce our chances of developing cognitive impairment as we age.[53]

Pro Tip: Note that to keep your mind sharp, you just need to learn a new skill. That's good news for those of you who are craft averse. You can learn to play an instrument, speak Italian, or rebuild a car!

Travel

In a study that examined creativity and fashion, the researchers discovered that fashion designers who lived and worked abroad produced more consistently creative work.[54] For those of us who don't get many opportunities to leave our state let alone the country, we can create the same kind of experience at home. Travel to a new place near you—a small town, a neighborhood or even a new restaurant. When you travel anywhere in your community—by foot, bike, or car—take a new route.

Climb a Tree

Physical activities that engage proprioception and the cerebellum—like climbing a tree or walking on a balance beam—improve our working memory.[55] Proprioception is our ability to know where a body part is and activate it without having to look. Of course, you can get a similar benefit from trying balancing workouts at the gym or scaling a climbing wall.

Bonus: Exercise

We know that exercise boosts creativity[56] and productivity. Art Kramer, a neuroscientist at the University of Illinois, found that just 45 minutes of exercise three days a week increased the volume of the brain.[57] Writers are famous for walking. William Wordsworth composed entire poems on his legendary long walks. Rumor has it that Agatha Christie created her complex plots on long walks with her dogs. Try taking a daily trek in nature or walking around the block between tasks.

Game Play Tips

- Start small. Often, when we try something new, we want to leap to the head of the class. We don't want to just knit a washcloth, we imagine creating a fancy sweater. When we don't succeed, we feel like failures—and that can reinforce negative neural pathways. But if we can start with a small step—ten minutes of yoga, a few minutes of balancing exercises each day, knitting a scarf—we can experience success and change our brain!
- Persist past small obstacles. Learning new things can be hard! But the most growth comes when we work to overcome the tiny obstacles, like working to master a difficult measure on the piano. See the practice—and the small obstacles—as a significant and beneficial part of the journey.
- Enlist your inner superhero! When we cannot imagine ourselves conquering a climbing wall or doing aerial yoga, it can be helpful to imagine what our inner superhero would do. Check in with your secret identity: how might The Amazing Innovator or The Flying Ninja tackle this challenge?

For the Win

Change can be hard. But the shifts and changes suggested in this quest might be a fun way to expand your brain and improve your life! Enjoy!

47. REFRAME BLOCKS

If you're not prepared to be wrong, you'll never come up with anything original.

— Ken Robinson

What do you do when you have a project that seems to be going nowhere? How do we work with feeling stuck? In the book *Designing Your Life*, authors Bill Burnett and Dave Evans frame that experience this way, "And don't worry about being stuck. Designers get stuck all the time. Being stuck can be a launching pad for creativity."[58]

Whoa! Now that's a reframe! With this point of view, being stuck can actually SAVE your project and make it better than ever. But how? The authors suggest that readers use mind mapping (discussed in the "Introduction" on page 11) to discover new ideas[59]—and then connect the ideas in unique ways to create even more fun possibilities. We can do the same thing with our writing—mind map possible solutions to a problem until we find solutions.

In an interview I did with Donna Gephart about her book *Olivia Bean, Trivia Queen*, she mentioned how spending time brainstorming helped her find the perfect idea:

> I often give myself time goals. e.g., I'll write/scribble for two hours, then I don't get up or check e-mail or Facebook until those two hours are up. Two days before NaNoWriMo began, I had no idea what my new book would be about. So I told myself I'd try to come up with ideas for two hours. At one hour and fifty-eight minutes, I scribbled these words: "Olivia Bean, Trivia Queen." The next day, I knew Olivia loved trivia. The day after that, I began writing about a girl who would do anything to get on her favorite show—*Jeopardy!* There's no substitute for putting in the time.

Wow! With a little time and the willingness to play with ideas, we can discover the perfect solution to our writing problem!

The Quest

The authors of *Designing Your Life* suggest that sometimes we get stuck when we're wedded to a path or working only with our typical solutions. In this quest, you'll reframe the experience of being stuck as a launching pad for creative solutions. Then you will reimagine new solutions for your problem.

Reframe

When we get stuck, it's tempting to blame ourselves and then look for a reason. What did we do wrong? Why are we unable to move forward on this project? How can we be so dense? Instead of trying to figure out why we are blocked or blaming ourselves for being blocked, look at the block as an opportunity. Being stuck can be a precious gift—a chance to rethink, reimagine, and restart this project.

Create a sentence that helps you see this situation as an opportunity and feel grateful for it:

- *I'm grateful I have the opportunity to make this a better project.*
- *I'm thankful that I can reimagine this story.*
- *I'm excited by the possibilities of what this could become.*

Reimagine

Brainstorm possible new directions or solutions to the project. Use lists, mind-maps, free writing, or any other tool that helps you get to a new place. Ask, *What if...* and follow the answers wherever they go. Be open to new formats, genres, audiences, writing styles, and content. Mix and match answers for unique mash-ups—maybe your romance novel could become a Zombie Regency romance with a twist of mystery? Or your talk on networking tips could become an interactive workbook or class.

Create

Once you discover a direction that feels energizing—follow it. If you get stuck, don't worry. Try again.

Game Play Tips

- The key to this quest is mindset: see the problem as an opportunity. Try to catch yourself when you slip back into a negative mindset about experiencing an obstacle. Then reframe again: *I've landed on a launching pad, not run into a roadblock.*
- Albert Einstein said, "We cannot solve our problems with the same level of thinking that created them." Adopt the mindset of your secret identity, your favorite superhero, or your ideal reader—and see if that helps you come up with new solutions.
- Consider hosting a brainstorming party. Invite your allies (see "26. Identify Your Allies" on page 91) and other open-minded friends and colleagues. Get together and imagine possibilities.
- See "73. Boost Your Imagination" on page 220 for more concrete brainstorming suggestions.

For the Win

Sometimes it's all in how you look at it. Walt Disney's first animation studio, Laugh-O-Gram Studio, went bankrupt. But he started again and launched the Disney Brothers Cartoon Studio in California, which became the famous and successful Walt Disney Studio. At 3M, a failed adhesive became the brilliant idea behind sticky notes. What will you launch from here?

48. OVERCOME PERFECTIONISM

Perfection is the voice of the oppressor, the enemy of the people. It will keep you cramped and insane your whole life, and it is the main obstacle between you and a sh***y first draft.

– Anne Lamott

As perfectionists, we're often trying to do two different things at once: create and perfect. These two goals conflict with each other. When we create something new, such as writing a draft, our goal is to get words onto paper. We're exploring ideas or telling a story. It doesn't help us to analyze our story or revise our writing in the midst of getting it written. It's when we edit a draft—when we are reviewing it for content, flow, and grammar—that we can work to improve it. When our perfectionist brain takes over, we squish the two tasks together and try to do both at one time. Of course this doesn't work. It's difficult to perfect a draft when we're trying to get our ideas down on paper.

Recently, I started running. I am slow, but I like the challenge. I've noticed that most runners don't agonize over each step, wondering if they are doing it right. That would be silly. No one can analyze a race and run it at the same time. Runners put one foot in front of another, moving quickly (or slowly, in my case) toward their goal.

Writers can learn from runners. Don't think so much. Just move forward. Get the words down on paper. You can fix it later.

This quest will help you overcome perfectionism and write.

The Quest

Step One: Set a Goal
What do you want to accomplish today? Write a paragraph? Tell a scene from your story? Write a query letter? Write down your goal.

Step Two: Lower Your Expectations
Review your goal. Is it doable? Is it small enough to fit the time you have allotted for writing? If you need to edit your piece in addition to writing it, then schedule extra time so that you don't have to do both tasks at once.

Step Three: Set Your Intention

In the book *Better Than Perfect*, Elizabeth Lombardo suggests that we do better when we are fueled by passion, working toward what we want to experience versus avoiding what we fear.[60] Writers often avoid writing because they fear that their work won't be perfect. Instead of worrying about making the work perfect, choose one of the following intentions and use it to fuel your writing time:

- Purpose: What do I want to accomplish with this? Who will I help?
- Passion: What am I excited about in this story or idea?
- Energy: What energizes me in this story or project?
- Curiosity: What am I curious about?
- Engagement: What ideas or parts of the story engage me?

Step Four: Write!

Using your specific intention, write.

Game Play Tips

- Try out intentions until you find the one that helps you overcome perfection and write. You may need a different intention for each project or stage of a writing assignment.
- Regular journaling can be a helpful antidote to perfectionism. Writing three rough pages a day will help you get in the habit of writing without expectations.
- Whether writing is your profession, a vital part of your work, or an avocation that you hope will become your profession, it's tempting to take it too seriously. Approaching your writing as play can help you overcome perfectionism and level up your writing. Next time you write, try to make it playful and fun. Use a new method for expressing yourself or experiment with a new format.

For the Win

Most perfectionists have been coping with this personality trait since childhood. Changing your behavior will take time and practice. Be patient with yourself.

49. EXPLAIN WELL

Dwell on the beauty of life. Watch the stars, and see yourself running with them.

– Marcus Aurelius

Rejection happens.

Everyone who writes faces rejection—it's simply part of the territory. The freelance writer who pitches articles and books will have some of their ideas rejected, often multiple times. The novelist or nonfiction book author will have their queries, proposals, and manuscripts rejected by agents and publishers. And once published, authors will face readers and reviewers who dislike their work.

The key to persisting in the face of rejection is adopting an optimistic mindset. In the book *Learned Optimism*, psychologist Martin Seligman wrote about the importance of our explanatory style, or how we explain to ourselves why we experienced a positive or negative event. Optimists tend to view negative events as temporary, situational, and specific. For an optimist, a rejection letter is a single, isolated event. Things did not work out this time. It might be the editor or the timing. But they try again. Pessimists explain negative events as permanent, pervasive, and personal. For a pessimist, one rejection signals that they'll never get published. The pessimist takes the rejection personally (*I'm just not good enough. This always happens to me.*) and pervasive (*Nothing in my life goes right for me.*).

Adopting an optimistic mindset is the key to moving forward in the face of rejection and disappointment. This quest will help you practice a positive explanatory style.

The Quest

Step One: Evaluate

Your explanatory style shows up in the words of your inner critic as well as in how you talk about events in your life. If you've done some of the earlier quests that address the inner critic—particularly "27. Name Your Villains" on page 94, "38. Examine Your Thoughts" on page 128, and "40. Lasso of Truth" on page 132—you have collected plenty of data about your inner critic. Review that information to evaluate your explanatory style. If you need more input, take a look at how you reacted to one of the last challenging events that happened to you. It might have been a rejection, a disappointment, or an illness. How did you talk about it?

Step Two: Reframe

When rejection or disappointment happens, it can be easy to slip into the negative explanatory style. The goal of this quest is to catch yourself and flip the explanation. This requires that you notice when you fall into a negative explanation, shift it to a positive explanation, and then repeat it.

Notice. Next time something challenging happens, notice how you explain it. If you get a rejection, listen for internal messages that sound like this:

- Permanent: *This will never change. Nothing works out. I'll never get published.*
- Pervasive: *My whole life sucks. Nothing goes right. I always get rejected.*
- Personal: *It was my fault. Why me? Things don't work out for me. I'm just not good enough to be published.*

Flip it. Take the pessimistic message and flip it, trying a positive explanatory style. The following phrases might help you change the way you think about experiences.

- Temporary: *This shall pass. Things will get better. Tomorrow is a new day. Next time, I'll write a better query letter.*
- Specific: *Not everything is a good match. Maybe the editor was having a bad day.*
- Situational: *In this case things didn't go well. These things happen. It doesn't affect my whole life. With a different story or agent, I'll succeed.*

Step Three: Practice

Next time something challenging happens, practice using a positive explanatory style. Do this with everything, not just writing. When the cake you're baking for a family party flops, pass it off as a fluke. When you invite a new friend out for coffee and they refuse, don't take it personally. And when the book proposal you submit gets rejected 25 times, take a deep breath, remind yourself that the next place might be the right place, and try again. Keep practicing this until it becomes a habit.

Game Play Tips

- You can also use your journal to discover when you slip into a negative explanatory style. If you practice daily pages (see "35. Journal to Boost Productivity" on page 114), review them for any signs that you are explaining challenging events in a way that is permanent, pervasive, and personal. When you see this happening, rewrite the story with a positive explanatory style.

- This quest can be used to reflect on the stories we tell ourselves about past events or experiences. If you've consistently understood a past experience using a negative explanatory style, try flipping it. Rewrite the story using a positive explanatory style in your journal. See how it feels. Then practice telling it to yourself and others. (See "40. Lasso of Truth" on page 132 for another quest on examining and flipping personal stories.)
- Our explanatory styles are often deeply ingrained in us. We may not even notice when we slip into a negative explanatory style. Enlist your partner or a trusted friend to help you notice when you slip—and then help you flip to the positive.

For the Win

Adopting a positive mindset takes time and patience. But the payoff is great. You'll feel more resilient when it comes to writing and end up feeling happier all around.

PART FOUR: DITCH DISTRACTIONS

50. Evaluate Distractions
Examine what distracts you and the practices you use to successfully manage distractions.

51. Complete Unfinished Business
Deal with the tasks and meetings that distract you.

52. Create Systems
Create a system for coping with recurring unfinished business.

53. Learn to Single Task
Practice clustering similar tasks and focusing on a single task at a time.

54. Assess Multitasking
Determine when multitasking helps or distracts you.

55. Utilize Shiny Object Syndrome
Learn how to harness the power of new ideas.

56. Stay on Track
Discover how to stay focused when you're hit with distractions.

57. Manage Social Media
Commit to technology free writing time.

58. Claim Idle Time
Use down time to renew your energy.

59. Take an Inspiration Sabbatical
Use inspiring breaks to increase creativity.

60. Play with Transition Time
Create an energizing transition between tasks to get more done.

50. EVALUATE DISTRACTIONS

At painful times, when composition is impossible and reading is not enough, grammars and dictionaries are excellent for distraction.

– Elizabeth Barrett Browning

When I started Dream Keepers, my teen writing group, we met at a church. Because it was a busy congregation, we often gathered at a table in the middle of a basement hallway. As the teens wrote about their lives, children and adults walked by, chatting and laughing. I could barely concentrate—and I was teaching, not writing.

I invited the teens to my house to work. As we sat around my dining room table, writing about our dreams for the future, one of the teens said, "It's so quiet here." Another added, "I know! I can barely work. I need some noise!" As the group talked, a split emerged: about half of the teens loved writing in the quiet environment while the others missed the noise of the busy church. I learned something crucial that night: what one writer finds distracting might be another writer's white noise.

Before we can eliminate distractions, we need to discover what distracts us and how we usually cope with distractions. In this quest, we'll review our best and worst writing times, examine common distractions, and explore the practices we use to focus and write. The other quests in this section offer tools for overcoming specific kinds of distractions, such as the negative internal voice or social media. This quest provides crucial information for working through this section of the book.

The Quest

Before you begin the quest, it's helpful to understand the various types of distractions. Most distractions fall into the following categories:

Internal Distractions

Unfinished Business: Personal or professional tasks that you need to complete

Shiny Object Syndrome: Ideas, projects, or opportunities that emerge while you are writing

Doubt or Fear: Internal anxiety about everything from deadlines to work quality

Emotional Drama: Both positive and negative deep feelings that demand attention

External Distractions

Virtual Connections: Phone calls, texts, social media, and email

Physical Connections: Colleagues, family, housemates, animals, repair people, mail carriers, friends, strangers, and more

Work Space:
At home or office—piles of papers, books, laundry, and anything else in your workspace that needs to be done
In public—people, conversations, noise, food, drink, and more

Media: Television, movies, music, games, social media

Note Common Distractions

Review your best and worst writing sessions and note common distractions. If you've worked through previous sections of this book, you may already have a record of your most and least productive writing sessions. In "21. Discern Your Best Practices" on page 77, you reviewed your writing sessions and recorded your best writing practices. In "23. Find Wisdom in Weaknesses" on page 83, you detected your least helpful writing practices.

As you review your writing sessions, you might discover that during your least productive writing times you were juggling multiple tasks, including answering texts and checking incoming phone calls. Pay special attention to distractions that popped up repeatedly. If you tend to regularly get distracted by a friend who texts you right in the middle of your writing session, note that. But if a writing session went badly because a child was home sick from school or your cat jumped on your computer, that's less significant unless it happens regularly.

Note Helpful Practices

Look again at your writing sessions and note the practices that helped you manage distractions. This may include actions like writing at a quiet space away from home, journaling before you write, or turning off your cell phone. Find a place to record these practices so that you can return to them when you need them.

Review the Results

When you're done with this quest, you will have two lists: common distractions and helpful practices. Review both lists and note which distractions repeatedly challenge you despite the practices you've put in place.

For example, I have a multitalented client who works in many creative mediums including writing essays and poetry and painting. He loves new ideas and projects, and he often feels inspired to work on a new project when he is writing. No matter what practices he put in place, he continued to be distracted by what we called "shiny object syndrome." We worked together to find a tool to help him honor his desire to create and finish the writing project. Once you know what distractions pull you from your central work, you'll be able to look at the quests in this section and choose the ones that will help you most.

Game Play Tips

- If you have trouble recalling what distracted you and how you dealt with it, observe your writing practices for the next week or two and use that information to create your lists.
- Review the list of villains you created when doing the quest "27. Name Your Villains" on page 94 for hints about your regular distractions.
- Keep your list of distractions and practices handy so that you can add to it as you experience new distractions and develop tools for overcoming them.

For the Win

Here's the good news: you've already developed practices to help you overcome distractions and focus. You've got a game plan that works—most of the time. And here's more good news: this section of the book is chock-full of great quests to help you overcome distractions and write more. Try out quests until you find the practices that can help you ditch those distractions and finish your work.

51. COMPLETE UNFINISHED BUSINESS

If you spend too much time thinking about a thing, you'll never get it done.

– Bruce Lee

In the middle of writing about our protagonist's fight with her mother, we remember that we need to purchase a birthday gift for our own mom. We open Etsy and search for the perfect necklace. As we write our weekly blog post, we notice the piles of unwashed laundry in the corner of our bedroom. We plow ahead, trying to ignore the smell of unwashed socks.

Unfinished business pulls our attention away from our writing. Sometimes we give up on writing and attend to the tasks in front of us, hoping to cross the item off our to-do list. At other times, the tasks just ping at our concentration, like an unchecked phone text or email, and impair our focus. The solution? Take on the unfinished business quest—and complete all those loose tasks.

In this quest, you will take care of as much of your unfinished business as possible. Yay! Freedom awaits you!

The Quest

You're going to feel so good when you've completed this quest! But first— make sure you have plenty of time set aside to work through the unfinished tasks. Don't take on this task when you're approaching a big holiday or deadline. And while it can feel amazing to tackle and complete all of your unfinished tasks quickly, it may not be realistic to do so. Be gracious with yourself.

Step One: List It

Create a list of all that stuff you've been meaning to do that you never get around to. These are the tasks that haunt you in the middle of the night and when you should be writing. You know, your annual physical, the piles of laundry in the basement, and paying that parking ticket.

Step Two: Complete or Schedule

Schedule a chunk of time to wrap up unfinished business. This might mean finishing incomplete tasks like writing and sending thank you notes for your wedding (was that really two years ago?) or finally recycling your outdated computers. You might also need to schedule appointments for things like detailing the car, cleaning your teeth, or getting new gutters put on the house. Once you've completed or scheduled tasks, you will feel relieved.

Step Three: Make Time

After completing a majority of your unfinished tasks, create time each week or month to deal with the items on your to-do list and any other unfinished business that you've been putting off. You can make this easier by creating a system to take care of unfinished business—which is the aim of the next quest.

Game Play Tips

- Review your list of unfinished business and consider delegating some of the tasks. Perhaps you can afford to hire someone to clean your house or order your groceries from a delivery service.
- Recruit your allies (see "26. Identify Your Allies" on page 91)! Checking in with a buddy can help us tackle and complete unpleasant tasks. Find a colleague to be your accountability partner for unfinished business.
- Be proactive: Schedule appointments as far in advance as possible. Set aside time in your calendar to deal with regular tasks, such as laundry. You'll learn more about this in the next quest, "52. Create Systems" on page 165.

For the Win

You'll notice that the minute you clear off most of your unfinished business, more will show up. That's okay. In the next quest, you'll be setting up systems to help you deal with it. When you have a system, you won't need to worry about your unfinished tasks—you'll have a plan for taking care of them!

52. CREATE SYSTEMS

Everything must be made as simple as possible. But not simpler.
                                                – Albert Einstein

Unfinished business happens. My theology professor liked to tell us that we'd die with our inboxes full.

Anyone who has ever tried to go on vacation knows how true this is. No matter how hard we try to clear everything out and finish all of our tasks before vacation, we end up leaving home with tasks undone.

Everyone has regular appointments, payments, and meetings that must be scheduled, paid for, and attended. We also have work and writing tasks that must be done. Often, we deal with these as they occur to us, when they pop up on our computer, or show up on the calendar. But being reactive taxes our brains and takes away our ability to focus on writing tasks.

This quest will help you be proactive. You'll create a system for dealing with regular appointments, tasks, and unfinished business, so you don't have to worry about completing these tasks when you are writing or working on a big project.

The Quest

Step One: Map the Big Picture
In this step, you'll create a giant list of your responsibilities. You can start with a mind map or create a list on a spreadsheet.

Recurring events, appointments, and payments: Take a look at your schedule and life and list any appointments, payments, and meetings that must be scheduled, paid for, and attended. This category includes items like regular networking group meetings; health and beauty appointments for you, your family, and pets; and online tool renewals (like domain names).

Tasks and meetings: Review your schedule and lists of tasks and note unfinished tasks. This might include assignments for work or writing, meetings or workshops, and special events.

Social, family, and recreational events: Review your calendar and add any events that you regularly do with family and friends.

Step Two: Create Scheduling Systems

Organizers tell us that containers provide the solution to preventing the junk that clutters up our dining room table or dresser. In a similar way, we need a container for the items on our task list. Choose a tool that works for you—a plain notebook, a sheet in your calendar, or a phone application like Google Keep or Todoist. This is where you will store or schedule the tasks that come up regularly.

Automate: Circle anything you can automate. For example, instead of reacting to the email notes to renew a domain name, can you automate your renewal? Automate them now.

Advanced scheduling: Note anything you can schedule 6 months to a year in advance. Schedule what you can right now. Set aside a chunk of time in your calendar to schedule future appointments and add a note about what you need to schedule. You may also wish to set up reminders in your scheduling system.

Weekly scheduling: The remaining items on your list may need to be addressed weekly. Add a block of time to your weekly schedule that's dedicated to addressing the regular business that comes up.

Step Three: Create an Unfinished Business Container

No matter how thoroughly you try to contain and cope with tasks and deadlines, you won't be able to anticipate everything that could pop up. Unfinished business happens. Create a space on your paper or electronic to-do list to record unfinished business. Set aside time to deal with these items during your weekly scheduling period.

Game Play Tips

- Play around with different options for addressing events. While you might be happy with your paper calendar, try out an electronic tool to remind you of recurring appointments and tasks.
- When unfinished business does threaten to pull your focus away from writing, treat it like you would an errant thought while meditating. Jot it down and return your focus to your work.
- Whenever you have an opportunity to schedule a task ahead of time, take it. For example, most dentists and hair salons like to schedule your next appointment before you leave. This benefits both of you—the business secures you for another paid appointment and, because you are selecting your appointment in advance, you get to choose the best time for you. And even if the time turns out to not work, you'll have an opportunity to reschedule the appointment when you receive your reminder.

For the Win

Systems make life easier. And the best systems are the ones we design for ourselves. With your own system for organizing and managing your life, you'll be able to get so much more done!

53. LEARN TO SINGLE TASK

Lack of direction, not lack of time, is the problem. We all have twenty-four hour days.

– Zig Ziglar

Jugglers amaze me. They keep multiple items moving at one time, in front of a crowd of fans, and without breaking their focus.

Whether you're a full time writer, an entrepreneur who's writing a book, or a professional starting a blog to promote your business, you're probably juggling more than one big project. On top of that, thanks to the recent social media explosion, most of us also blog, tweet, pin, post on Facebook, and more. Add to all of this the other stuff we do in life (exercise, eat, connect, volunteer)—well, no wonder it's hard to focus on a single task.

Many of us turn to multitasking to get things done. We think that focusing on multiple tasks at once might double or triple our productivity. Wrong!

Let's start by learning what multitasking really is. When we move back and forth between multiple tasks, psychologists call it "context switching." Jordan Grafman of the National Institute of Neurological Disorders and Stroke says it's not multitasking but rapid toggling. According to Bob Sullivan and Hugh Thompson, the authors of *The Plateau Effect*, "One study showed today's office worker gets only eleven continuous minutes on a project before interruption. But much worse than that, it takes twenty-five minutes for them to return to the original project after interruption."[61]

And some of us never do. The authors of *The Plateau Effect* reported on another study that said after we get interrupted, we move to some other task 40% of the time.[62] If you're writing a book, that means that almost half the time, after you stop to check that incoming text or email, you're not going back to working on your book. You've moved on to another task.

Though many claim to be able to effectively juggle multiple projects at once, they can't. No one can. Research shows that people who self-define as efficient multitaskers are actually less competent at doing multiple things at once.

The solution, though, is simple: single tasking. Do one thing at a time with as few external disruptions as possible. This quest will give you the opportunity to practice single tasking.

The Quest

Step One
Divide your day into chunks and then assign a single task to
each chunk of time.

Step Two
Unless your task is online social networking, during every other task—
especially writing—turn off the technology that distracts you from your
current work. This might be the internet, email, or your phone.

Step Three
Set a timer for 10-15 minutes and do the single thing. If it's writing,
then write. When you finish, take a quick break. Give yourself a reward.
Repeat the "focus, break, reward" pattern until you've come to the end
of your time chunk. Then take a break and move on to the next task on
your schedule.

Step Four
After you complete an entire day of single tasking, check in with yourself. How did that work for you? Did you get more done? Or do you feel
better when you have a little more distraction for part of your day? Again,
evaluate and revise your life accordingly!

Game Play Tips
- You may be plagued by brain drama; random thoughts racing
  through your brain, tasks to complete and ideas to work on.
  Gently flick away those thoughts, add them to your to-do list, or
  write them down in an idea journal.
- It takes practice to focus. Remind yourself that you have time
  scheduled to do all of the things you're worrying about and then
  turn back to your writing. You might have to do this fifty times
  the first day, but it will get better.
- When it's time to reward yourself, choose power-ups that are
  designed to help you renew your energy and focus, like exercising, walking in nature, or doing something repetitive like
  folding towels.

For the Win
Any time you've been able to ditch multitasking, overcome monkey mind,
and focus on writing for a set amount of time, you have won the game. As
you work on single tasking, you'll strengthen the muscles that help you
focus and you'll get better at doing it.

54. ASSESS MULTITASKING

Multitasking is the opportunity to mess up more than one thing at a time.

– Anonymous

I've been a proponent of single tasking for years, and yet multitasking tempts me. I'm most often guilty of media multitasking—turning on a movie or video while doing a less-fun task, like creating invoices. The problem? While the movie makes the boring task more fun, it also slows me down. And I make embarrassing mistakes—like getting names wrong on letters and emails.

New research by Cyrus Foroughi, a PhD candidate from George Mason University, suggests that small interruptions decrease our ability to write well.[63] And multitasking can be understood as purposely welcoming interruptions. In two studies, participants were asked to outline and write an essay. In the first study, some were interrupted at regular intervals. In the second study, they were interrupted at random times. But the result was the same: those who were interrupted wrote less and scored lower than their peers. Clearly, interruptions make writing more difficult. In addition, interruptions and multitasking lower one's performance ability:

- When students received a 2.8 second interruption during a test, their errors doubled. When they received a 4 second interruption, their errors quadrupled.[64]
- Media multitasking—reading a book while watching television—results in poor performance on both tasks.[65]
- Task-switching can lower your IQ an average of 10 points, about the same as if you smoked marijuana or stayed up all night.[66]

Yikes.

So is there ever a time when multitasking works? Yes—people can effectively juggle multiple tasks when all but one of the tasks are automatic. A parent can hold a conversation with one child while feeding another. Teachers answer questions about an assignment while passing out the morning snack. And who hasn't enjoyed listening to music and sipping an iced tea while driving down the freeway? But as soon as one of the additional tasks requires more focus, then multitasking fails. So when a student asks the teacher to look at their paper or the road becomes icy—then it becomes more challenging. We don't perform well when we are juggling more than one focused task at a time.

This quest will help you evaluate when, where, and why you multitask. Once you know that, you can use single tasking when you're working on the projects that require the most focus. And you can save your multitasking for the times when it doesn't impact your performance!

The Quest

Review
When do you multitask? Review your life for times when you multitask and make a list. It might look like this:

- **Commute.** *Complete phone calls to prospective clients.*
- **Cooking.** *Watch television while making dinner.*
- **Research.** *Keep an eye on Twitter while researching potential book markets.*
- **Write.** *Check Facebook when I get bored or frustrated with writing.*
- **Connect.** *Keep an eye on my phone and answer texts during meetings.*

Evaluate
For the next week, pay attention to these multitasking sessions and evaluate them. Does multitasking affect your productivity? Does it affect your accuracy? What are you getting out of multitasking? Does it improve how you feel about doing less-desirable tasks? Do you feel like you are getting more done when you multitask? Or does multitasking—or really context switching—give you a break during difficult tasks?

Reflect
After evaluating these multitasking sessions, note what kinds of multitasking negatively impact your productivity or effectiveness. Note also how multitasking improves your experience of a task. For example, I often watch television shows on Netflix while chopping vegetables for soup. The practice makes the task more fun—I catch up on my favorite shows and create a healthy meal!

Address
If you use multitasking or rapid context switching when you hit a difficult patch in your writing, consider how else you can deal with your frustration. For example, when you don't know how to write a scene, you might check email or social media and not get back to writing that day. Next time, consider taking a short, renewing break—like walking around the block—and then return to writing. You might journal about the problem you're having, addressing possible solutions. Or you could simply skip the tough part and come back to it later.

Practice
Choose one or two of the tasks that are negatively affected by multitasking. For the next week, commit to single tasking when you're working on those projects. For example, if you need to research blogs to guest post on, set a timer to research markets for 10-15 minutes—without also watching television or monitoring Facebook.

Game Play Tips
- Use this quest any time your work productivity slips. It can help you identify when multitasking isn't working for you.
- As a coach, when my clients continually use practices that slow or stop their productivity, I ask: "What are you getting out of it?" When you have difficulty changing your multitasking habits, it might be helpful to consider how multitasking is benefiting you—even when it isn't increasing your productivity.
- Consider how you might benefit from using single tasking in your regular writing practice. When did single tasking help you the most? When did single tasking help you increase your productivity or accuracy? How will you make this a regular habit?

For the Win
We win when we can make our habits work for us rather than against us. In this quest, you discovered when multitasking makes tasks go faster and when it interrupts your focus and slows your productivity. Now that you know what works and what doesn't—you can choose when, where, and how to multitask!

55. UTILIZE SHINY OBJECT SYNDROME

Perhaps when we find ourselves wanting everything, it is because we are dangerously close to wanting nothing.

– Sylvia Plath

I happened upon the phrase "shiny object syndrome" (see "50. Evaluate Distractions" on page 160) when working with a client who had trouble focusing on his current project because there was always a shiny new idea or project waiting for him.

Our minds move fast and the ideas tend to come when we are busy working on something else. Unfortunately, these ideas do not respect our boundaries, so while we're working on the novel, ideas for the nonfiction book or an article or a business plan pop up. Often the lure of a shiny new idea can take us away from the work we're doing right now.

You might have shiny object syndrome if:

- You flit from idea to idea.
- You have so many ideas, you have trouble choosing one.
- The minute you commit to an idea, you find several better ones.
- When you settle down to work on a single project, new ideas fly to you like bees to pollen.
- You can lose a morning or a few days to exploring a new idea.

You probably know when shiny object syndrome will hit. For most of my clients, it attacks them when they're working on their most-challenging writing assignments. Shiny object syndrome also shows up when we're working on projects that are less exciting—maybe compiling that year-end report for work or indexing a book.

This quest will help you learn how to record and entertain those ideas so they don't derail you from working on your central project. After you complete the task, you'll have a system to deal with shiny object syndrome.

The Quest

This quest is divided into three levels. The first level will help you to develop a system for dealing with the ideas that pop up while you are writing. The second and third levels offer two different ways to entertain shiny objects within your workweek.

Level One

What do you do with those shiny new ideas that hit you while you're working? Do you chase them, jot them down in your phone, or hope you'll remember them later? Many of my clients find shiny object syndrome so distracting because they worry if they don't tackle that idea right now, it will flutter off to another writer, like a butterfly in search of a fresh flower. I've heard at least two writers, Anne Lamott and Elizabeth Gilbert, suggest that the muse can be fickle like that, taking our good ideas to someone else when we choose not to respond in the way she is accustomed to!

Instead of worrying about losing those ideas, create a system to record your bright and shiny brilliant new thoughts. Many writers carry index cards around with them, while other writers simply note ideas in their phone either in a notes application or by sending themselves an email. Other writers keep an idea notebook or idea files. The method doesn't matter. You need a system that allows you to record and access notes at any time and from anywhere. Use the system that works best for you and your lifestyle.

Once you decide on a system, try it for a few weeks. Each time a shiny new idea pops up in your head, record it. Don't dwell on it, research it, or start a new project. Just note it in your idea file. Once you've done this for a few weeks, the system should start to feel normal to you.

Level Two

Choose a second task to work on in tandem with your current creative project. During your writing session, set a timer for 15-45 minutes and work on your current project. Give yourself a five-minute break. Maybe take a power-up during the break—walk around the block, fold towels, or dance to fun music. Set your timer for 15-45 minutes and work on the second task. Toggle back and forth between tasks in 15 to 45 minute blocks for your entire creative time.

At the end of each session and at the end of the week, reflect on how this went. Did working on the second task help dampen your case of shiny object syndrome or did you have even more ideas hit you?

Level Three

Schedule time to dig into one of your shiny new ideas. At the beginning of the week, set aside 45 minutes to play with a new idea. When a new idea hits while you're working on your current project, write it down (using your system of recording shiny new ideas) and remind yourself that you've already scheduled time this week to dig into a new idea. Think about using this shiny object time as a reward for getting work done.

Game Play Tips

- Try each level for multiple writing sessions to get a clear sense of how each tool works for you.
- For Level Two, it can also work to assign each creative project a separate section of time, like a day of the week or week of the month.
- Level Three can also be treated as an artist date. Take time to explore a shiny new idea at the library, in a class, or at a retreat.
- Recruit your allies (see "26. Identify Your Allies" on page 91)! Friends and colleagues can be a good sounding board and source of information when it comes to considering new projects. Share and reflect on your new ideas with your allies. They might be able to help you figure out what to do with these sparkling ideas.

For the Win

When you learn to collect and record shiny new ideas, they can become the bread and butter of the creative life. Instead of distracting you from the projects you need to finish, the new ideas can be used to add richness to current projects or spur new ones. And by having a system to collect shiny new ideas, you don't have to worry about losing track of them.

56. STAY ON TRACK

There is a light at the end of the tunnel, but the way out is through.
– David Allen

Ever start one task and end up doing something entirely different? Imagine you're getting ready for company, and are straightening up your living room. After you put away DVDs and set the remotes on the coffee table, you return a half-eaten bag of chips to the kitchen. You notice the cupboard is a mess. So you clean it out. When you toss the stale chips, the garbage overflows. You take out the trash, and notice that the floor is littered with dead leaves. You take out a broom . . . and on it goes. Hours later, if you're lucky and you can find your way back, you'll finish getting the living room ready for company.

The same thing can happen with creative projects. We're in the middle of writing a scene or section, when a research question pops up. We note it in our project journal and keep writing. But then the question comes up again, and we don't want to waste a whole morning drafting something that won't work, so we open our favorite search engine. We find a page with an answer to our question and realize this would be a great place to guest blog. We compose a letter to the blogger, introducing ourselves and asking for her guest blogging policies. Once we've done that, we think, "Maybe I need guest blogging policies!" We compose them. Halfway through, we remember, "I promised my followers a blog post this week." We open a new document and write down some ideas. We get hungry and search for cookies or chocolate. But we're out of treats, so we head to the store. Do we ever get back to the writing?

This quest will help you to stay on track, no matter what distractions appear!

The Quest

The goal of this quest is to interrupt the interruption. When we're distracted by an idea or action that will take us off our current task, we purposefully put on the brakes and turn back to the task.

First, acknowledge that "applying the brakes" is a necessary step in the writing process.[67] Once you notice that you're chasing down a new idea or embarking on a different task, you might think, *Oh crap, there I go again, getting distracted.* Instead, accept that distractions happen. Everyone gets pulled off task. It's part of the job. It's how we deal with these distractions that counts.

In the book *Improv Wisdom*, author Patricia Ryan Madson presents lessons from the world of improvisational theatre. One of the maxims is, "Stay on course." In that chapter, she invites readers to ask themselves repeatedly during the day, "What is my purpose now?"[68]

As you're writing this week, notice when you're feeling pulled off task. Gently ask yourself, "What's my purpose now?" If you've set aside the time to write, then your purpose is to write. It is not time to tackle unfinished business or rearrange your office or clean out the pantry. Keep a notebook by your desk or a file open on your computer to jot down the other tasks, worries, and ideas that threaten to pull you off course. Then go back to your work.

Game Play Tips

- If the maxim, "Stay on course" or the question, "What's my purpose now?" doesn't work for you, try another one. Some of my favorites are: Stay in your lane. Keep calm and stay the course. Focus.
- If you know you're tempted to be distracted by social media, consider working where you don't have access to the internet, or purchase a program that can temporarily block your access to the internet or to any site you find tempting.
- Use this tool in all areas of your life. Any time you get off task—while cleaning up the living room, cooking dinner, or answering email—gently remind yourself to stay on course.

For the Win

Like in meditation, we can easily get pulled off course by thoughts and distractions when we write. But with this quest you've strengthened your ability to stay the course. And by doing that, you've no doubt increased your ability to finish things—like paragraphs, sections, and even projects. Yay you!

57. MANAGE SOCIAL MEDIA

Distracted from distraction by distraction.

– T.S. Eliot

Before my annual social media sabbatical, I contemplated hiring someone to take care of updating my social media sites while I was on break. I chose to save money and do it myself. That meant checking email and posting on social media sites during my time off.

Though the actual tasks took no more than five hours to complete, it catapulted me back into work mode. After answering emails and checking in on Facebook and Twitter, I worried over clients, obsessed about work situations, and fretted about events around the world. Though I was taking daily adventures with my family, I had difficulty being present. The experience reminded me why I take a social media sabbatical every year.

Here's the thing: I love social media. Through social media, I can connect with interesting authors and thinkers throughout the world. Because of social media, I've met fascinating people and learned many new things. Email, video chat, and social media platforms make my job possible—and easier.

Technology almost demands that we multitask—at the very least, using our smart phones to check in on social media and email when we're waiting in line, or using our commuting time to catch up on phone calls. Here are statistics that clarify how much our technology rules our days:

- The average person checks their inbox 15 times a day.[69]
- Most people check their phone 46 times a day.[70]
- We spend over four hours a day on our phones.[71]

But this type of multitasking costs us time and attention. Here are some of the costs associated with checking email and social media:

Deciding What to Post Taxes Our Brains

Spending time on social media can lead to cognitive overload. As we surf online and decide what to like, share, and post—our brains get overwhelmed. Instead of thinking about our current writing projects, we're worrying what people will think about the political meme we posted. Our brain does not perform well on our key tasks because it's distracted by our social media activity.[72]

Checking Email Lowers Our IQ

The Institute of Psychiatry at the University of London published a study on infomania—dealing with the relentless push of information from emails, cellphone calls, and instant messages. They found that when people were bombarded with email and phone calls while performing a creative task, their IQ decreased 10 points, which was similar to what happened when people smoked marijuana.[73]

Did you get that? If you're writing your book and take a break to check your email, it affects you like you stepped out to smoke a joint. Holy smokes!

What does this mean for you? That smart phone that keeps buzzing? The Twitter feed popping up on your screen? Even the IM on Facebook? They're killing your ability to write.

When it comes to ending addiction, many programs recommend complete abstinence. In this quest, you will commit to technology free writing time or temporary abstinence. Afterwards, you'll reflect on how writing without social media and phone notifications affected your writing.

The Quest

Schedule

Give yourself a block of interruption-free time to write. It doesn't have to be a whole day. It can be two hours on a Saturday afternoon, 30 minutes each morning before the rest of the family wakes up, or ten minutes before bedtime. No matter the amount of time you can grab, take it and commit to it.

Before you start writing, sign off social media, turn off your phone, and close your email and web browsers. If you find giving up technology to be difficult, start small—30 minutes of writing time.

Prepare to feel the internal tug to check email, visit Twitter, or text a friend. Instead of giving in, acknowledge the desire: *Hey, I hear you, this is hard, it's tempting to want to play on social media.* Then remind yourself when you will go online: *Just write for another 20 minutes, and you can check email.*

Reflect

After each session and at the end of a week, make a note of these things:

- In what ways did shutting off technology improve your productivity? Maybe you got more done in less time or you were able to think more creatively.
- During your technology fast, what technology did you want to use the most: social media sites (specify which ones), online search sites, email, or phone?
- Did anything frustrate you about writing without being connected to social media?
- How will you use this tool going forward?

Game Play Tips

- Go beyond the obvious and turn off anything electronic that might interrupt you, including your fitness tracker, alarm reminders, and text messages.
- Decide ahead of time on a signal that your family or housemates will recognize as "Writer at work" and leave you alone. This might be wearing a special hat or putting a "do not disturb" sign on your door.
- Schedule time to connect with people via phone, email, and social media. Many writers use technology like the office water cooler—stopping over to Facebook every time we need a break or texting a friend between work tasks. Instead, schedule time to connect via technology, just like you schedule time to write. Then, give yourself energy boosting breaks—take a walk, fold the laundry, or play with an animal.

For the Win

We don't need to be slaves to technology. With this quest you determined how technology could serve you in getting stuff done and connecting with others. Good for you.

58. CLAIM IDLE TIME

When I am constantly running there is no time for being. When there is no time for being there is no time for listening.

– Madeleine L'Engle

Several weeks ago, I set aside a Saturday to work on my business plan. I packed up my computer, calendar, and books and headed to the library. I spent the next two hours staring at my lists, mind maps, book outlines, and business goals. I dug into dozens of projects and felt…exhausted. I left the library feeling discouraged. My inner critic launched into her usual rant: *You don't work hard enough.*

When I spoke to my coach about it, she had an insight: I'd misdiagnosed the problem. I was busting my butt. I didn't need to work harder. I needed a break.

Lately, I've become aware of how little time I have to simply be idle. It's a rare moment when I'm not working, writing, talking, texting, teaching, coaching, caring, cooking, or cleaning. And when I do have a free moment, I tend to use it to check one of my digital devices. I'm not alone. Americans spend 16 minutes of every hour on social networks.[74]

I've written repeatedly about how writers need idle time to develop their ideas. At a writing conference, I heard Sara Paretsky talk about how her best books emerged from fallow periods, when she had the time to listen for the voices of her characters.

Recent research backs up this anecdotal evidence. In a 2009 study led by Professor Kalina Christoff, University of British Columbia Dept. of Psychology, researchers discovered that when our minds wander, two parts of our brain get activated: our default network (the part associated with routine mental activity) and our executive network (the part linked to complex problem-solving). Christoff and her team concluded that when we get stumped by our work, it might be helpful to focus on simple, routine tasks and let our minds wander.[75]

If you're struggling to find new ideas, develop your story, explore a character's voice, describe a setting, or simply get something down on paper, you might need some idle time. This quest will help you get up and do…nothing!

The Quest

Set aside at least an hour for this quest. Several hours could be better.

Remove

Turn off your devices (scary but you can do it!) and, if you live or work in a busy place, leave it.

Engage

Spend time engaged in a mindless task. Here are some ideas.

- Walk
- Nap
- Sweep
- Swim
- Ride in a car, train, or bus
- Chop vegetables
- Weed
- Paint
- Bake

Reflect

Afterwards, reflect on how the quest went—were you able to daydream? (If so, record your daydreams!) Did you have enough time? Was the task you chose sufficiently mindless to allow you time to dream? What would you tweak for your next daydreaming session?

Game Play Tips

- Daydreaming takes practice! Repeat this quest as often as needed to connect with your inner visions. We get better at being idle the more we do it. Not only that, the practice can deliver deeper benefits once we've done it a few times.
- Watch out for your villains and inner critics—they tend to attack when our minds are idle. If this is a problem for you, it can be helpful to listen to uplifting music during the first few times you do this quest. Or revisit some of the quests in "40. Lasso of Truth" on page 132.
- This quest is also a power-up—something you can do whenever you get stuck to strengthen your writing muscles! Woot!

For the Win

Many people like to say, you can't get something for nothing! In this case, they're plain wrong. Idle time benefits us in so many ways. Think of it as a car trip for your brain (in fact, car trips can be one of the best places for daydreaming)! Whenever you feel overwhelmed by work or life, do nothing.

59. TAKE AN INSPIRATION SABBATICAL

Writing is not a matter of time, but a matter of space. If you don't keep space in your head for writing, you won't write even if you have the time.

– Katerina Stoykova Klemer

For weeks before the spinning beach ball of death took control of my computer, locking me out from everything, it made several short appearances. My computer repeatedly warned me: "Your startup disk is full. You need to make more space available on your startup disk by deleting files." I moved files to an external hard drive and deleted unused programs. I might as well have been trying to empty the ocean with a bucket.

In the midst of one late-night moving session, my computer said something like, "I don't have the space to do this but, if you want to do it, I'll keep trying." And so it did. I could not get the computer to stop trying. The guy I called from the manufacturer could not figure out how to make it stop. The tech guy who came over finally halted the crazy spinning by sneaking in the computer's back door and moving out some of those big files that had trapped the computer in a seemingly endless cycle of pointless activity.

My computer guy let me in on a secret: your computer needs to have 15-20% of its space free to operate. So when it's stuffed with words, programs, and photos—it gets stuck.

That got me thinking about my writing brain. I write first thing in the morning, before I've checked email, but my brain isn't just sitting there, waiting to spout out brilliant dialogue. Instead, the thoughts scurry around the hamster wheel in my head: *What do I need to sign for the kids? Is my lunch date still on? When do I see clients? I hope I can get the editing done today. What else did I say I'd do? I think I owe my friend a text. I should check Facebook.* You know how it goes. I don't have enough free space in there to focus on reading a book let alone writing one.

According to a recent study by Angelika Dimoka, director of the Center for Neural Decision Making at Temple University, when the prefrontal cortex gets overloaded with information, it shuts down. This part of your brain makes decisions and regulates emotions. When it closes up shop, you're more likely to make stupid mistakes or bad choices.[76]

You might be thinking, *Well, that's just how it is!* No, it's not. Here are some signs that your brain might be on overload:

- Forgetting deadlines & appointments
- Feeling agitated while relaxing (*I should be doing something*)
- Difficulty concentrating on writing or other projects

- Trouble focusing on and remembering what you're reading
- Rapidly hopping from idea to task and back again
- Feeling exhausted or being unproductive at your most productive times of day

All of us—especially writers—must clear out our overcrowded brain. Don't let too much bad news or poor writing clog up your brain space. Keep clear of negative voices. Complainers, criticizers, and naysayers all pollute your precious brain.

So what's the solution? We can buy a big old external hard drive for our computer and offload some of our information stash onto that. But we cannot buy more brain space. When your brain's start up disk is full (and whose isn't full?), don't wait until you crash—get sick or have a full-blown meltdown.

This quest will help you to clear brain clutter so that you can generate ideas and write.

The Quest

Set aside time for your sabbatical. Start small—maybe a single day or even an afternoon each week. During this time, you'll be taking a break from distracting noise and input. You will also be exposing yourself to inspiring experiences.

Eliminate

Take a sabbatical from external noise. Eliminate any distraction you can: television, radio, social media, phone, and email contact. Consider taking time away from family, friends, and regular daily responsibilities. (I know! I'm asking for a miracle!)

Immerse

The sabbatical is defined as much by what you add in as what you take away. Spend the time experimenting with inspiring practices and input. What sorts of reading, music, art, and movies nourish you and your creativity? Consider taking a field trip to a place that you find enriching—a bookstore, concert, art museum, or nature center. Do activities that you find inspiring—perhaps dancing, walking, cycling, making art, or attending concerts.

Reflect

At the end of your sabbatical, consider:

- What brought you the most inspiration?
- What voices are you longing to hear again? What distractions did you miss?
- What toxic or troublesome habits and voices can you let go of?
- What voices are you not looking forward to hearing again?
- Reconnect with the voices and input that work.

Game Play Tips

- Play with the elements of your sabbatical: time of day, day of the week, habits you let go of, actions you take on, whether you stay home or escape to a retreat center. Evaluate each sabbatical and work to put together several variations that can help you get inspired depending on your needs and mood.
- If you're social and get energy from other people, consider taking your inspiration sabbatical with one of your friends or allies (see "26. Identify Your Allies" on page 91).
- Consider adding a sabbatical from distractions as a regular part of your weekly, monthly, or yearly schedule.

For the Win

Each time I take an inspiring sabbatical, I get flooded with ideas and return to work with more energy than I thought possible! I wonder why I don't schedule sabbaticals more often! Now that you've had a taste of the sabbatical, why not schedule a few more?

60. PLAY WITH TRANSITION TIME

The human soul can always use a new tradition. Sometimes we require them.

– Pat Conroy

When my children were little, I'd read to their classes once a week. Invariably, I'd arrive when the students were in the middle of something—finishing a project, having a snack, or writing in their journals. The teacher would lead them in a transition ritual to help them move their attention and their bodies from the project to the carpet for story time. Sometimes the students would sing their cleanup song as they put away their supplies. At other times, they would put away their work and try to be caught sitting quietly so that they could be called to story time. Whatever the ritual, the effect was the same: the transition time gave the children an opportunity to shift their focus from their current activity to the new one.

As a freelancer who juggles multiple projects, including my own writing, transition time helps me to clear my mind and renew my energy for each new task. When I'm done with my writing task for the day, I quickly set my writing goal for the next day—so that I will know what my subconscious needs to be thinking about—and then I take a break. In the book *Organize Your Mind, Organize Your Life*, the authors suggest using physical stress-busting activities like walking, stretching, or lifting weights between activities in order to perform better on the next task.[77]

In this quest, you will experiment with different activities to help you transition from one task to another or from the end of your workday into your evening.

The Quest

Review the power-up tools in the appendix and list five activities that you believe will help you let go of one project and transition to a new one.

Experiment

Transition time. This week, experiment with taking transition time between writing tasks. At the end of the week, reflect on what transition activities worked the best for you. Then, make a plan to use transition time regularly.

Wrap-up time. It can also be helpful to add wrap-up time to each writing session. Schedule time at the end of each session to wrap up your current work on a project. If possible, create a to-do list or a plan for the next writing session. If you have some idea what you will be writing about the next day, your subconscious can do the work for you!

Over and out. Add a transition period to the end of your workday, especially if you work from a home office. This allows you to leave the work of the day in your office or at your desk so you can be fully present with yourself, your partner, or your family for the evening.

Game Play Tips

- If you do multiple blocks of work time with breaks in between, as in the Pomodoro method (see "64. Take Five" on page 198), these energy restoring breaks will help you get even more done while you work.
- It's tempting to use social media or answering email as transition time between projects. Unfortunately, using social media or another task as a break can distract us and drain our energy. Try to find transition activities away from your desk.
- If you have an accountability partner, messaging each other between tasks can be a good way to transition from one task to another.

For the Win

Tiny rituals can transform our days. Instead of carrying worries from project to project, having a transition time can help us move forward and focus on the next task. And here's a bonus idea: when you finish a task, why not stand up and cheer for yourself. If you work with others, get in the practice of offering high fives after each small win!

PART FIVE: OVERCOME OBSTACLES

61. Diagnose Writer's Block
Review and evaluate experiences of writer's block.

62. Write the Best Bits
Discover and write the most engaging parts of your work.

63. Give Up Something
Let go of a commitment or project to find time to write.

64. Take Five
Try short bursts of writing.

65. Stop in the Middle
Stop in the middle of a paragraph, scene, or chapter to make returning easier.

66. Plan Accurately
Study past writing projects and learn how to estimate project time frames.

67. Exercise Writing Muscles
Play with writing exercises to bust blocks.

68. Revise Forward
Revise a scene or section as a tool for writing forward.

69. Make Small Shifts
Create a list of possible tiny shifts and try one.

70. Play with Poetry
Try poetic techniques to enrich your writing.

71. Ask the Magic Questions
Ask questions to reconnect with your purpose for writing the project and discover your next step.

72. Take a Scavenger Hunt
Take a scavenger hunt to spark new ideas.

73. Boost Your Imagination
Try tools to help you increase your ability to imagine.

74. Improve Your Writing
Practice exercises designed to stretch your writing skills.

75. Try Sticktoitiveness
Use a butt-in-chair tool to stick to your writing project.

76. Reframe Rejection
Create a plan to deal with rejection.

77. Write Fifteen Minutes a Day
Try out multiple ways of writing for fifteen minutes a day.

78. Wait Productively
Create a plan to make waiting time work for you.

61. DIAGNOSE WRITER'S BLOCK

There's no such thing as writer's block. That was invented by people in California who couldn't write.

– Terry Pratchett

Writers agonize over writer's block. When we're having little luck writing, we blame writer's block. When we're writing well, we worry that writer's block will attack us, interrupt our progress, and keep us from making our deadlines. We develop intricate habits to prevent writer's block from happening, fearing that if we miss one step, writer's block will freeze us.

But here's the thing: the experience of writer's block—or having difficulty getting words on paper—is most often a symptom and not the disease. When we encounter writer's block, it's a nudge from our subconscious that something in our writing isn't working. When we look at writer's block as a symptom, we have the opportunity to discover a way to move forward with our writing. The key to overcoming writer's block is to diagnose it and then fix it.

In this quest, you'll put on your scientist hat, collect the data about your experiences with writer's block, and then analyze it. This quest can and should be repeated whenever writer's block strikes.

The Quest

Step One: Review
Take some time over the next week, and look at the last three times you experienced writer's block or procrastination. Ask yourself these questions:

- What happened? Write a short summary of what happened at the time.
- What was going on with the writing? (Is there something in what you're working on that doesn't feel right? Is it the structure, characters, dialogue, research?)
- What was going on with you? (Did something internal—such as a false belief about yourself or the writing—interrupt your writing?)
- What was going on with your environment? (Did something external, either online or in person, interrupt your writing?)
- How did you handle it?
- Did the solution work?
- How could you use the skill you used here the next time you get stuck?

Review the same period of writing and consider three times when you were productive. Ask yourself the very same questions:

- What happened? Write a short summary of what happened at the time.
- What was going on with the writing?
- What was going on with you?
- What was going on with your environment?

Step Two: Evaluate

Evaluate the data. No doubt you already have some specific ideas about what's making it challenging to write right now—and what you need to succeed. Review the information you gathered and then make two lists:

- What practices, emotions, tools, and other circumstances help me write?
- What practices, emotions, and other circumstances make writing difficult?
- Once you've written down all the general items, zero in to this particular period and project and try to figure out what factors are making writing challenging right now.

Step Three: Get Practical

You now know what makes writing work—and what gets in the way. You also know what is not working in this specific project. Brainstorm ways to schedule and complete writing when you are most successful. Research and imagine tools to help you overcome the specific blocks that are getting in the way of your writing. Get help to overcome the block: find a book, hire a coach, or ask a friend. Don't let a concrete issue interrupt your writing.

Game Play Tips

- If you find it difficult to recall what happened last time you experienced writer's block or writing success, track your writing sessions for the next few weeks. After each session, jot down notes about what happened, what helped you succeed, and what threatened your progress. Or, check out your journal entries for "21. Discern Your Best Practices" on page 77 or "23. Find Wisdom in Weaknesses" on page 83.
- It's tempting to blame yourself for writer's block, saying things like, *I'm just not disciplined.* Or *I'm easily distracted.* Don't. Dig deeper until you can find a more specific explanation, such as: *When I have so many other responsibilities, I have difficulty being*

disciplined about writing. Or, I struggle with creating dialogue, and I need to do it for this project.

- This section—Part Five: Overcome Obstacles—is packed full of quests to help you overcome specific kinds of obstacles. The quests in "40. Lasso of Truth" on page 132 will help you address any challenges you have with attitude or the inner critic. Use these quests to help you solve the issues you discovered in this quest.

For the Win

When we consistently solve writer's block instead of worrying about it, we overcome it more quickly. In time, we won't need writer's block to show up in order to discover what's not working. We'll know what's not working, fix it, and avoid the drama of nasty writer's block altogether.

62. WRITE THE BEST BITS

Leave out the parts that readers tend to skip.

– Elmore Leonard

Vladimir Nabokov, author of *Lolita*, wrote all of his novels on 3 x 5 index cards. Each day as he began his writing period, he would shuffle the cards until he found a scene that he had energy to write and start writing from there. When the scenes were done, he rearranged the cards until he discovered the novel's order.

Crime fiction author Lori Rader-Day wrote her first novel while working at a demanding full-time job. Writing over lunch breaks, after work, and on weekends, she made sure her book was interesting enough to engage her even when she was tired. Thriller author Chelsea Cain loves to create challenging puzzles for her characters to solve—which keeps her jazzed up to write every day.

For this quest, you'll skip the boring parts, and discover how to find something that piques your interest.

The Quest

Review your book notes or outline and choose a scene or a section that you find engaging. It might engage you because it is: puzzling, funny, romantic, interesting, or delicious in some other way.

If you're struggling to engage with the scene or section of your book, try one of the following tools to make it more interesting. After spending a writing session with one or more of these tools, evaluate how it went.

Fiction

- What's the character's inner conflict in the scene? How does that drive the action? How can you show that?
- What's the external conflict in the scene? How can you show that through action and dialogue?
- How can you jump into the middle of the conflict, whether it's internal or external?
- Is there a character change you can highlight in this scene?
- Change the point of view of the scene and see if that reveals something to help move the story forward.
- Can you shift the style of the scene? Can you use more dialogue, action, or description to make the scene more interesting?
- Can you enhance the scene by borrowing a technique from a different genre? Would infusing a scene with techniques from a romance novel help (e.g., misunderstanding, overhearing, roman-

tic triangle)? Would adding a mystery make the scene more intriguing?

- Are there sensory details that will make this scene feel delicious to you and the reader?
- How can you show the character doing something dangerous, questionable, or just plain stupid before they reflect on it?
- Play with setting. Send your characters to a place that challenges them and pulls out the conflict within or between them.
- Ask your characters what they want and then follow them into unique, hilarious, or dangerous places.
- Explore your characters' emotional center by giving them way too much to handle and seeing how they react.

Nonfiction

- Explain a fact, practice, or background information in a unique way using a story, metaphor, or simile.
- Tell a story about a person or organization that illustrates the information or process you are explaining.
- Find a detail that will make your story more interesting.
- Create an emotional connection with the reader by showing how an experience affected the person or organization.
- Present the effect that a process, practice, or product has on the people who do it or buy it.
- Search for an interesting fact, idea, or story to hook your reader's interest for this part of the book.
- Think about how you could use data to make your point.
- Consider how you could use an unfolding mystery to present your information.
- Is there a creative way to present this information that makes readers excited to learn it?
- How can you make the information interactive? Could you create a quiz, activity, or chart that helps the reader understand and engage with the material?
- Write the part of the piece that puzzles you or that you still have questions about. How can your curiosity drive the piece?
- Write for a specific reader in mind—how will this part of the book help them understand the topic or move forward with their life?
- If you're not sure what section to write, choose something you know a lot about and can write easily. How can you add excitement to this information?

Game Play Tips

- When you choose your scene or section, pay attention to your energy level. What excites you? What engages you? What stirs your passion?
- If the tool you tried didn't work, try another tool. Keep trying different tools until you find the ones that work for you. Know that you may need different tools depending on what section or scene you're working on.
- Treat this writing session like you would treat an experiment—play at it. Have fun. Don't take yourself or the writing too seriously.

For the Win

Once you write all of the fun parts, you might concur with Elmore Leonard and decide to leave out anything readers would skip!

63. GIVE UP SOMETHING

How could we keep [this creative power] alive? By using it, by letting it out, by giving some time to it. But if we are women we think it is more important to wipe noses and carry doilies than to write or to play the piano. And men spend their lives adding and subtracting and dictating letters when they secretly long to write sonnets and play the violin and burst into tears at the sunset.

– Brenda Ueland

Several years ago, USA Today Snapshots® posted this question: "What would you give up for a year to fulfill the No. 1 item on your ultimate to-do list?" 65% of people said social networking, 56% would give up their cellphone, and 53% would give up time with friends.[78]

How about you? What would you be willing to give up to write your book? Would you be able to let go of some or all of your social media time?

The choice to let go of a daily or weekly activity to write doesn't have to be all or nothing: either I write the book or I spend time with friends. Consider giving up an hour or two each week of socializing, social networking, meetings, or another commitment to work on your writing.

In this quest, you'll do just that: give up something good to spend time with something better—your writing or other creative project.

The Quest

Review your schedule and reflect on what you might let go of in order to write. Pay special attention to the time you spend on social media, since that can snap up so much of our day. Be ruthless—look at every single thing you do and ask, "Is this more important than my writing? What would happen if I let it go and wrote? Could I at least let go of half of the time I spend on that activity?" Here are some activities to consider giving up. Note that all of these activities are valuable and meaningful—but sometimes it may be necessary to give up an activity you love and value to focus on an important project:

- Volunteer commitments (committees, task or service groups, organizational work)
- Social or work groups (book groups, networking meetings, craft groups, critique groups)
- Social commitments (regular coffee, lunch, or dinner gatherings; social outings)
- Entertainment (television, gaming, online socializing; concerts, plays, or sporting events; outdoor activities and sports)

- Home maintenance projects (Could you hire someone to help you with cleaning, cooking, laundry, shopping, dog walking, snow shoveling, or childcare?)
- Conferences or educational events (Annual conferences, weekend workshops, weekly classes)
- Work projects (Could you let go of any work projects that are low-paying and time consuming?)

Choose one item from the list above to let go of for at least two weeks and write during that time. After two weeks, reflect on how it went. Did that extra chunk of time help you write more? Do you want to continue using that time to write?

Game Play Tips

- This tool works best if you're writing something you feel passionate about and can see its purpose, despite any obstacles you face.
- Expect to be challenged by friends, family, and colleagues, especially if you are giving up time with them to write.
- Once you've successfully let go of one activity, if you still feel like you need more time, consider letting go of another time-consuming activity.

For the Win

In order to do the big things in life, we sometimes need to give up something else we value. It might even be another writing project that's eating up the time and energy we'd rather devote to the writing we're truly passionate about. But once you've opened up the space to focus on what matters to you, life will feel more expansive.

64. TAKE FIVE

You don't have to see the whole staircase, just take the first step.
— Martin Luther King, Jr.

In the Netflix sitcom *Unbreakable Kimmy Schmidt*, Kimmy spent 15 years underground in the bunker of a doomsday cult. When she's rescued, Kimmy heads to New York City to begin a new life. Along the way she offers bits of wisdom from her days in the bunker, including this one from episode two: "You can stand anything for 10 seconds. Then you just start on a new 10 seconds." Kimmy flashes back to the bunker, where she turned a crank—to no purposeful end—for 10 seconds at a time.

I immediately thought of writing—and all of us who fight to overcome our procrastination habit. When it's time to write, procrastinators will do anything to avoid writing. Clean the toilets? Sure! Pay the bills? No problem. Attend a committee meeting? Sign me up! When we procrastinate, our house may be cleaner than ever, but we're no closer to finishing our project and achieving our dream of publishing a book.

In the book *Mind Gym* by Sebastian Bailey and Octavius Black, the authors recommend that readers overcome procrastination by taking a five-minute start.[79] And that's exactly what you'll do in this quest.

The Quest

Overcome procrastination by shortening the time of your writing session. Set a timer for five minutes and write. When the timer beeps, think about how it feels to write. If you're up to it, set your timer for another five minutes.

Level Up

Once you can sustain five-minute writing sessions, try a ten-minute session. Increase your time until you get to the ideal length for your writing session.

How long is the ideal writing session? The Pomodoro Technique, developed by Francesco Cirillo in the late 1980s, suggests that people work best in 25-minute increments. In *The Power of Full Engagement* by Tony Schwartz and Jim Loehr, the authors recommend 45-minute intervals.[80] Choose the length of time that works for you.

Game Play Tips

- Add a power-up break between timed sessions to renew your energy.
- Boost the effectiveness of this quest by participating in a timed sprint with another writer as well as the clock. How many words can you write in 20 minutes?
- Whenever procrastination tempts you or distractions overwhelm you, go back to the 5-minute timed writing session until you can sustain a longer session again.

For the Win

When we take on hard tasks in small chunks—like five-minute bursts of writing—we can overcome procrastination and finish projects. As we level up, we get stronger and increase our endurance. We're able to write for longer chunks of time—and get more done.

65. STOP IN THE MIDDLE

People who say it cannot be done should not interrupt those who are doing it.

– George Bernard Shaw

Who can imagine stopping in the middle of eating an ice cream cone, making love, or arguing a point? When I get to the good part of a book, I hate stopping—even if it means postponing work or staying up past my bedtime. But stopping in the middle of a writing task—especially if you're at a juicy part—can help you write more tomorrow.

Psychology researcher Bluma Zeigarnik found that not finishing a task in one sitting is good—because we tend to remember the tasks we were working on when we stop in the middle. Her idea that we remember unfinished tasks better than finished ones is called the Zeigarnik effect. Being able to stop in the middle of writing a paragraph or scene means we'll have a natural place to start the next day. When we get to our desk, we can pick up where we left off. Brilliant!

Zeigarnik might have named the practice, but Hemingway did it first. In a 1935 article for *Esquire*, he said:

> The best way is always to stop when you are going good and when you know what will happen next. If you do that every day when you are writing a novel you will never be stuck. That is the most valuable thing I can tell you so try to remember it.[81]

We like finishing things. It feels good to turn in an assignment, wrap up a chapter, and then cross an item off our to-do list. But for this quest you will practice stopping in the middle of a paragraph, scene or chapter—and see if that practice helps you quickly get into your next day's writing session.

The Quest

For the next week, when you tackle your writing chunk, do not write to the end of a section. Instead, stop in the middle of an engaging or interesting paragraph. Make a note of where you stopped on your writing to-do list, so that you can think about what you'll be writing the next day. Then, the next time you write, pick up where you left off.

At the end of the week, evaluate this technique:

- What was it like to stop in the middle of a paragraph, scene, or chapter? Did you find it energizing or frustrating?

- How did stopping in the middle help you start your next writing session?
- Did this technique help you write more?
- Was this tool more helpful for particular types of writing?
- How might you use this tool as part of your regular writing routine?

Game Play Tips

- If you find you have trouble getting back into a task after an interruption, even a planned one like this, be sure to end your writing session by noting what you're writing and what you plan to do next. That will help you refocus when you get back to your desk. Check out the quest "30. Know the What" on page 102 for more information on how to plan what you will write.
- It can be helpful to plan mindless, repetitive activities immediately after stopping writing or at some point in the time between sessions (see "60. Play with Transition Time" on page 186). This will give your brain time to work out any issues you are having with your writing project.
- Track your success with using this quest. If it works regularly, then use it to overcome writer's block and increase your writing productivity.

For the Win

Delayed gratification can help us get stuff done. In this quest, we delayed the satisfaction of finishing a scene or a section in order to give us something to look forward to working on the next time we write. It's like freezing a movie in the middle—just before the exciting part. We can't wait to get back to work!

66. PLAN ACCURATELY

How did it get so late so soon?

– Dr. Seuss

If you're like me—bubbling over with ideas—you no doubt have more ideas for projects than you can handle at one time. For those of us who suffer from the planning fallacy—we underestimate how long it will take to finish a task—it's important to narrow down our choices even more.

Days start filled with so much possibility. As I plan, I imagine I can do more than humanly possible. More times than I care to admit, I've started a load of clothes only to find them three days later, turning moldy in the washing machine. Yuck!

I've been done in by what scientists call the planning fallacy.[82] (Don't worry, you can't catch it.) But know that you probably suffer from it, too. Here's a quick quiz. Think back on past writing, work, and home projects:

- Have you ever underestimated the time it will take you to complete a task?
- Have you ever underestimated the external resources you need to complete a task (e.g., money, research time, outside experts, editors, marketing professionals, etc.)?
- Have you ever created a project plan without taking into account external circumstances like illness, meetings, computer problems, and writer's block?

No doubt you answered yes to at least one of those questions. (If you said no to all three questions, send me an email. I want to learn your strategies!)

In a 1994 study[83] of psychology students, they calculated how long it would take them to finish their senior thesis for both best-case and worst-case scenarios. Guess what? Most students took longer to finish their paper than their estimated worst-case scenario.

Why? Psychologists have several theories for why we suffer from the planning fallacy.

- We tend to want to impress others, so we make optimistic estimates. (When participants made anonymous estimates, the planning fallacy disappeared.)
- We tend to take credit for things that go well and blame outside forces for setbacks.
- We focus on the project in isolation and forget about factors such as sickness, other projects, external delays, and so forth.

The problem? When we fail to plan well, we end up rushing through the end of the project, sometimes pulling all-nighters. Worst-case scenario? We miss our deadlines.

The fix? Keeping detailed work records can help us plan better. When we record our work time, noting any delays, we can create more realistic plans for future writing and editing projects.

In this quest, you'll review past writing projects, reflect on the information you gather, and use that data to create a Task Estimation Tool, a chart that will help you plan your next writing project.

The Quest

Review

Review three past experiences with work or writing projects:

- How many hours did it take you to complete the project?
- How much calendar time did it take to complete the project? (E.g., It might take you six hours to write a proposal, but the project took a total of two weeks because you needed to wait for data from an outside source.)
- What external delays did you encounter while working on the project? (E.g., waiting for an editor to review your manuscript, waiting to hear from a resource.)
- What internal delays did you experience? (E.g., exhaustion, illness, writer's block.)

Reflect and Create

Reflect on the data you collected. If you were a project manager for a work team, you'd take all of this information into account when estimating deadlines and setting schedules.

Create a Task Estimation Tool. This is a chart that provides your best time and resource estimates for common writing and editing tasks. For example, you might note that when doing a revision of your writing, your average speed is 4 pages an hour. Next time you need to estimate how long a project will take, you can use the chart to help you plan well.

Plan

Put your new information to work by planning. Start small by planning a small project or a week of work. This will allow you to try out the accuracy of your Task Estimation Tool. After completing a few days or weeks of this, you'll get a sense of what sort of plans work best for you.

Game Play Tips

- When you estimate a new task, always add a bit of extra time to your estimate—just in case you need it. You may not use it, but when you do need it, you'll be thankful to have it!
- Update your Task Estimation Tool after you complete new tasks. Add the task and information about time and resources to the tool. If you have an experience that takes longer than you had hoped it would, reflect on why that might be so—and add the information to your tool. All of this data will help you plan future writing projects and avoid the planning fallacy.

For the Win

The planning fallacy might make it difficult to create workable plans, but this quest teaches us how to use our experiences to plan realistically. Instead of missing deadlines, we'll be cruising through a project and meeting our deadlines without drama.

67. EXERCISE WRITING MUSCLES

Writing is like a sport. You only get better if you practice.

– Rick Riordan

I've titled this quest, "Exercise Writing Muscles," but I'm not talking about running or practicing yoga, though exercise and other repetitive tasks (folding towels or knitting) can help you overcome writer's block. I'm talking about using writing exercises to play with words.

As a nearly full-time professional writer, I rarely do writing exercises. Because I depend on my writing to pay the bills, I feel guilty spending time on non-billable writing. But when I teach writing to children at the library, it's my job to teach and model writing exercises. In those moments, when I write the biography of a famous book character or create a winter haiku, I often discover new ideas for my current work in progress. Doing writing exercises helps me access my creativity and gain skills that I can use in my billable writing work.

In this quest, you'll purposely play with words as a tool for busting through writer's block.

The Quest
Try one of the following writing exercises. Afterwards, reflect on how this tool impacted your writing.

Interview a Character
I have frequently used dialogue to explore challenging feelings or situations. Instead of analyzing the difficulties of a new relationship or reviewing my feelings, I ask questions of the situation or emotion and then write the first response that comes to mind. If you're writing nonfiction, you might try creating an imaginary dialogue with a potential reader or the subject of your work.

This is also a good technique for connecting with characters in your novel. When an unplanned character shows up or starts behaving badly, write down your questions and answer as fast as you can without giving it too much thought. Trust your intuition and the voice of the character to provide the answer. Helpful questions for both feelings and characters include:

- What are you doing here?
- What do you have to teach me?
- In what ways are you a blessing to me?
- What is your role in the story? (or the story of my life?)
- What do I need to know about you?

Found Poetry

Artist John Morse created haiku poetry using found phrases from ads and posted them on the streets of Atlanta. In a project called Curbside Haiku, Morse created safety messages and images that the New York Department of Transportation installed across the city.[84]

Look for phrases on street signs, bumper stickers, and billboards. Collect snippets of dialogue from overheard and remembered conversations. Once you have a list of phrases, create your own haiku using the phrases. Here are two examples from my student Elisha Branch:

> Bethel Baptist Church
> Rummage Sale is this Friday
> How much for Jesus?

> No child left behind
> Have faith in education
> I'm ten; I can't read.

Dream Journey

Reflect on a dream that intrigues you.

- Rewrite the dream, paying attention to recording sensory details. What sights, sounds, and smells do you recall? If you don't recall any, what would you imagine might be there?
- Are there characters in the dream that you're especially drawn to? Describe them. What did they look like? What do they value? What do they want?
- Underline bits of the dream that you think might make good scenes, metaphors, or images for a project you are working on. Write about how each might work. You might use sentence starters like, "What if …" For example, "What if my main character dreamt about fighting a dragon?" or "What if my main character fought a dragon?"
- Consider what might have happened in the dream before you started dreaming and after you woke up. If your dream was the middle of the story, how could the story begin and end?
- Does the dream, its characters, or metaphors contain a message for you or your readers? What might that be? Write it as a fortune from a cookie or a chocolate wrapper.

Object Lesson

Choose an old object from your home. If you don't have any, find a picture of an antique online. Imagine that when you touch the object, you are transported to its original time and place.

- Where are you?
- Who owns the object?
- What happens?
- How do you interact with the object?
- What does the object have to teach you?

Genre Play

Take a scene from your work in progress, an idea you need to communicate, a traditional fairy tale, or a story from your life, and write it in a different format or from a new point of view. Here are some formats to work with:

- Limerick
- Ballad
- Newspaper article
- Advertisement

- Tweet
- Horror story
- Romance
- Protest song

Game Play Tips

- To level up your writing skills, try doing one writing exercise a day during your usual journaling time or, if you're really stuck, work on one during your regular writing time.
- If the exercises in this quest don't thrill you, search for the writing exercises that work for you. For novelists, my favorite book of writing exercises is *Fiction Writer's Workshop* by Josip Novakovich. For writers of creative nonfiction, memoir, and self-help, check online resources, such as Wattpad.
- Consider taking a class or workshop to have the experience of doing writing exercises with others.
- It can be helpful to do a writing exercise with your own book in mind. Use your cast of characters or specific topic while working on the writing exercise.

For the Win

Writing exercises work because they tickle our brains with new ideas and information and help us to think and work in new ways. Who knows? Maybe you'll find the secret ingredient your story was missing,

68. REVISE FORWARD

The past is never dead. It's not even past.

– William Faulkner

Imagine that you're Stephen King, and you've just written *that* scene from Carrie—you know the one, the prom scene with the pig's blood. That key scene triggers a series of horrifying events—as it should, it's a horror story! But perhaps Stephen King wrote it the first time with Sue (the trustworthy friend) interrupting the prank, and the blood got dumped on her. Then what would Carrie and the others do?

Sometimes when our work is done, it's difficult to think about rewriting it or tossing it out, even when it doesn't work. In this quest, you will play with a scene or section of your current project in order to find a way forward.

The Quest

Play with a scene that doesn't feel quite right, and you may just find the perfect way to move forward. As they say, sometimes the best way to move forward is to rewrite the past!

But how? If you're writing a novel, try writing the scene using:

- A different point of view
- Just dialogue
- A flashback
- An additional character
- A new setting

If you're writing a nonfiction book, try writing the section using:

- An interactive element—a list, discussion questions, or quiz
- An anecdote from a client or history
- Evidence from research
- A concrete tool or exercise for readers to try
- A story, practice, or tool from your experience

Game Play Tips

- If writing in a new format or from a different point of view freaks you out, try starting with one of the last paragraphs you wrote and sharpening the prose. Just tinkering with the language for a bit can help you get into the groove and write forward.
- After writing the scene or section in a new way, reflect on how it went. Do you want to use anything from the new material? Did it give you any insight in how to move forward with your book?
- If you have trouble writing in a new way, recruit your secret identity and write in their voice for a paragraph or two. How does that offer you insight into the work? Does it help you move forward?

For the Win

Letting go of text that doesn't work can be hard. So can trying something completely new. In this exercise, you did both—and hopefully delving into a completely different way of writing this section of text helped you overcome a block and move forward with your writing.

69. MAKE SMALL SHIFTS

All great things have small beginnings.

– Peter Senge

In yoga, I notice that the small shifts yield big rewards. Tiny movements create aha moments. When I relax my shoulders, shift the angle of my foot, or lift my chin—the correct pose emerges. It feels right.

I've noticed the same phenomenon in writing. Often, a client comes to me with what seems to be a big problem:

- *When I finally get to the computer, I have nothing to say.*
- *I'm slogging through this long chapter. How do I make it sound better?*
- *I can't find time to write.*

In the midst of the coaching session, we talk about what small shift might nudge them toward success. The professor who can't figure out what to say imagines writing about the subject for a student, and suddenly the words pour out. The speaker struggling with voice tries out a different type of writing each day—essay, list, process—until he finds something that works. The therapist who can't find the time to write commits to jotting down ideas before work each day. These small shifts yield big rewards. They have the power to demolish writer's block and create space to write.

The mistake most of us make is to believe that writing success comes when we make a giant effort, taking a year off work to write our novel or working ourselves to death every single day. And effort matters. But for most of us who work as professional writers, this job is more like a marathon than a sprint. Yes, we must make an effort to reach success. But we must exercise that effort slowly, steadily, and over time.

In this quest, you will examine what isn't working, make a list of possible tiny shifts, and then try one of them.

The Quest

When something about the writing process or content isn't working, make a note of what's frustrating you or getting in the way of writing. For each frustration, make a list of possible tiny shifts. Here are some ideas to consider:

Habits

- Write at a different time.
- Write in a new place.
- Try writing with a different tool: computer, word processing program, or by hand.
- Ask a friend or colleague to join you in a write-in.
- Try timed writing.
- Write to music, white noise, or in silence.

Process

Change your approach to the process of writing.

- If you prefer outlines, write without one.
- If you love winging it, create an outline or a list of topics or scenes.
- Journal.
- Use a prewriting tool.
- Play with a writing exercise.

Content

Shifting a small part of the kind of content you create can help you break through blocks.

- Write on a new topic.
- Try a different genre or a trope from another genre
- Use a unique format. In *A Visit from the Goon Squad*, Jennifer Egan wrote a chapter as a Power Point presentation.
- Start in the middle of the story, jumping into the heart of the conflict.
- Write about the spectacular outcome your clients get.

Audience

Sometimes the small shift is within ourselves, thinking about who we are writing for.

- Write for a different market.
- Think about someone you know and care about and write to help them.
- Write for a younger version of yourself, when you needed this kind of a story or tool.
- Write as if this is a guide to help you navigate the current or next phase of your life.

Commit to making a single tiny shift. See what happens!

Game Play Tips

- Experiment with tweaking different parts of your writing habit, process, or content until one works.
- Recruit your strengths (in "22. Recognize Your Strengths" on page 80) to help you figure out what shifts to make. If you're detail oriented, perhaps your small shift is focusing on a tiny part of the project. Or if your strength is curiosity, perhaps your small shift is moving from making statements to asking questions.
- If you're unsure of what to tweak to get results, explore other quests in this section of the book or talk to colleagues about what has worked for them.

For the Win

Over time, writing a page a day can result in a book. In the same way, small shifts can create big results. Tweaking may seem trivial, but like taking small steps (as in "29. Take Small Steps" on page 100), these tiny tweaks make it possible for us to take action and achieve big goals.

70. PLAY WITH POETRY

Always be a poet, even in prose.

– Charles Baudelaire

Nearly every week, I teach poetry writing to children at the library. When they hear what we're going to do, many panic: *I can't do that! I don't know how to rhyme!* And my favorite, *But I don't love anyone like that!*

Last fall, I read a favorite, funny poem to the group while they colored. When I finished, a 2nd-grade boy said to me, "Wait, I thought you were going to read a poem."

"I just did."

"That was a poem?"

"Yes."

"That was good!"

"You sound surprised."

"Can you read it again?"

I read it three more times. Afterwards, we wrote poems together.

Reading and writing poetry improves all writing. Poetry teaches us to pay attention to what's happening in the world. With poetry, we learn to describe what we see with detail and craft. And because playing with poetry doesn't feel like real writing, it can sometimes help us overcome a sticky part in our work.

We don't have to be poets to use poetic tools to polish our storytelling. In this quest, you'll play with three ways you can add poetic techniques to enrich your writing. And of course, playing with poetry will also help you bust through writer's block.

The Quest

Review the following exercises and try one or more of them. When you finish, reflect on how it went. Did using the poetic tool help you write better? How satisfied are you with the result?

Add an Image

Poets use images or figurative language to help readers experience the objects, actions, and ideas in a piece. With metaphors, similes, sense words, and more, poets paint pictures for readers.

Your turn: Take one idea, object, or action in your current work in progress. Brainstorm images that might help you describe it. Then, revise the passage using one of the images.

Listen for Music

Poets listen for the rhythm of language. When they construct a line, they place rhymes, repeat sounds, and count the beats of each word.

Your turn: Read your current piece aloud. How does it sound? Would adding internal rhyme, alliteration (words that start with the same letter), or a different word improve the piece?

Say it Shorter

Poets describe the universe with just a few perfect words. Sometimes, they offer us only a glimpse into the world they are describing. But because they use juicy words, it's enough.

Your turn: Take a long sentence—25 words or more—and write it shorter.

Bonus! Play with Forms!

Try your hand at writing a haiku or a limerick. These simple forms can be challenging to use—but working through the puzzle will light up your brain and stimulate your thinking!

Game Play Tips

- Get help! Don't go this alone. Plenty of poetry tools exist, including rhyming dictionaries, idiom dictionaries, and the handy thesaurus.
- If poetry play helps you overcome writer's block, find a book of poetry writing exercises—even one written for children—and work through it. The exercises will make you a better writer. And who knows—you may just become a poet!
- Reading poetry—even if you don't understand it—will help you write better. If you're a newbie, try one of the collections referenced in the endnotes.[85]

For the Win

Poetry play can help even the most serious writer enjoy language, bust through blocks, and improve their storytelling. Revisit this whenever you need a little boost of rhyme and rhythm.

71. ASK THE MAGIC QUESTIONS

The starting point is a question.

– Alberto Manguel

Many of my friends talk about the Target effect. Has it happened to you? It's like this: we go into the store with a plan to purchase a specific item, usually something practical like hand soap. Somewhere in the middle of the trip, deep in the store, we notice that our cart is overflowing, and we can't remember what we came in to buy.

It's a bit like writing. (You knew that was coming.) When we start a book, we have an idea of where we are going. We know what we want to accomplish and why. And then five, fifty, or a few hundred pages in, we get stuck. The book doesn't seem to work, and like the Target shopper, we've forgotten why we're here in the first place. You wonder, "Why the heck am I writing this book?"

And asking that question will help you move forward.

When Meg Wolitzer spoke at Boswell Book Company to celebrate the paperback release of her novel, *The Interestings*, she gave advice for writers who get stuck. And who doesn't?

Here's what she said (paraphrased):

> *Stop writing. Go for a walk. Read a good book—even just a few pages. Once you have some distance, ask:*
>> *What was I trying to do with this book?*
>> *What should I do now?*

Wolitzer recounted how her editor does the same thing for her, asking what her vision for the book is and then holding her to that.

In this quest, you will use Wolitzer's questions to reconnect with your purpose for writing the book and to discover your next steps.

The Quest

The next time you're stuck with your writing, stop. Take a day or two off. Don't think about the book. Don't read other books with the thought that you might learn something about your book. Just do something mindless and fun: Watch a movie. Go for a walk. Clean your basement. (Okay, that's not fun, but it will get your mind off your project.) Then ask yourself the questions below and reflect on them.

Ask the Questions

Consider your current project. Ask: *When I started this book, what was I trying to do? What should I do now?* Write your answers in your journal. While you might have a single purpose for your book, you may end up with multiple ways to move forward.

Reflect and Plan

Reflect on what you wrote about your purpose. Review your work in process. Given this information, how might you move forward? Plan how you will continue or complete your project.

Game Play Tips

- When you consider what you wanted to do with this project, it may help to review your initial notes for the project or talk to any friends, coaches, or writing partners who you spoke with during the process of outlining your book or writing the initial chapters.
- You may experience a big gap between what you wanted to do with your project and what you've written. Perhaps you've written yourself into a new purpose, and that's okay—your book might have needed it. Evaluate what the gap means, and either commit yourself to the new purpose or create a path back to the original purpose. Review the quests "45. Define Your Purpose" on page 146 and "56. Stay on Track" on page 176 for more information about finding your purpose.
- You can use this quest to consider any part of a project, from a short chapter to the whole outline.
- A good editor or writing coach will hold your vision for you, keep it in front of you so you don't forget what you'd set out to do. This might be a good time to consult with someone to help you get back on track with your book.

For the Win

Congratulations on completing this course correction. Like the boat that got slightly off course thanks to the wind or rain, you have recalibrated and are sailing towards your goal!

72. TAKE A SCAVENGER HUNT

Creativity is a scavenger hunt. It's your obligation to pay attention to clues, to the thing that gives you that little tweak. The muses or fairies—they're trying to get your attention.

– Elizabeth Gilbert

Did you read the quote? According to Elizabeth Gilbert, author of *Eat, Pray, Love*, being creative requires that we pay attention to those inner tweaks, the moments when our curiosity is hooked and we want to follow our questions, just like Alice followed the White Rabbit down the hole. Remember?

> … when suddenly a White Rabbit with pink eyes ran close by her. … Alice started to her feet, for it flashed across her mind that she had never before seen a rabbit with either a waist-coat-pocket, or a watch to take out of it, and burning with curiosity, she ran across the field after it, and fortunately was just in time to see it pop down a large rabbit-hole under the hedge.
>
> In another moment down went Alice after it, never once considering how in the world she was to get out again.[86]

You've been there, right? Like Alice, you've seen something new or puzzling, and you must follow your curiosity wherever it goes, no matter the consequences. Recall the last time that happened to you and hold onto that feeling. Curiosity will hook you at the beginning of a project and keep you writing when you're tired, sick, and not making enough money!

When we get stuck or bored with our writing, it's often because we've sacrificed curiosity for certainty. Because we're juggling responsibilities and focused on meeting deadlines, we stick to what we know. We don't have time to get lost in a rabbit hole. To get unstuck, we need to find a way to pay attention and spark our curiosity.

In this quest, you will practice paying attention to the images, experiences, and ideas that tweak your curiosity and take scavenger hunts to spark new ideas.

The Quest

It's time to hunt for beauty, unique ideas, and fairies! You can do this in your ordinary life or you can take an adventure. The rules for each are the same: pay attention to what tweaks your curiosity and jot it down.

Pay Attention

Have you ever driven to a familiar destination and suddenly had no memory of how you got there? It happens to all of us, multiple times a week—and it's called autopilot. It can happen while driving, walking, working, or doing our daily chores. This quest is designed to help you avoid autopilot and pay attention. As you go through your days, note what's happening in your surroundings. Recall that feeling of being curious. Throughout the day, pay attention to what sparks that feeling. Collect images, actions, words, and stories to use in your writing. Only take pictures if you think you will need them. Instead, train your mind to make a memory. At the end of the day, practice creating a word picture in your journal by recording what you discovered. Remember, the muse is always at work, trying to get your attention.

Go on an Adventure!

When we do something unique, time feels like it slows down. We remember more on these adventures. To stir up our inquiring mind, we need to head out on a scavenger hunt for ideas!

- Go to somewhere that collects lots of information and ideas, like a library, museum, or bookstore. Browse until you get that zing!
- Take a guided tour of a factory, neighborhood, or historic building.
- Wander around your neighborhood, following only your curiosity. See what you discover.
- Take a day trip to a nearby community or town.
- Try a different route or mode of transportation. If you usually drive to work, take the bus! If you take the freeway, try the slower side roads.

Take an Online Tour

Go to a site where other people have collected lots of fun things and browse. Here are a few places I like.

Pinterest: Visit the site and browse the home page. Or, choose a category and see what shows up. You can also design searches and view the results.

Mix: This site allows visitors to search via topics and create collections of interesting posts.

Instagram: Because this site features photos and videos, it's a great place to find visual stimulation—and inspiration!

TED talks: TED collects talks from idea people in every field. Browse, listen, and browse some more until you find something that keeps you watching.

Reflect

Once you've taken a scavenger hunt or two, take a look at your notes.

- What themes emerged from your scavenger hunts?
- What do you still feel curious about? Circle the ideas.
- How can these ideas be worked into current projects?
- What ideas for new projects show up in these notes?

Game Play Tips

- I've listed just a few ways to pay attention and take adventures. But there are many more including viewing art, reading books, connecting with new people, and attending talks. Recall when and where you've had your best ideas and look for more of those experiences.
- Many authors report that regular journaling helps them reflect on their day and access the ideas that the muse has dropped in their lap. Check out the journaling tips in "Introduction" on page 11 and "35. Journal to Boost Productivity" on page 114 for tools on how to use journaling to mine your brain for ideas.
- After trying this quest, consider how you can seek curiosity in your everyday life.

For the Win

As a writer, your job is to pay attention and write about your wonderings. Hopefully this quest has reminded you how delicious that task can be! Whenever you get bored with writing, come back to this quest and take a scavenger hunt for ideas. Ask "What if?" and follow the answers, even if it takes you down a rabbit hole!

73. BOOST YOUR IMAGINATION

Logic will get you from A to Z; imagination will get you everywhere.
                                        – Albert Einstein

In 2006, I launched Dream Keepers, a writing program for children and teens in Milwaukee. Since then, I've taught at dozens of libraries, schools, and churches. In the past year, I've noticed that many of the young people have difficulty imagining. When I ask them to write a scary story, they write what they've seen in movies and on television. When I push them to create something of their own, they stare at me like I'm from outer space.

Creativity researcher Kyung Hee Kim, a professor at the College of William and Mary, discovered that creativity has decreased in children since 1990, along with the ability to imagine. She said that the data shows that "children have become less emotionally expressive, less energetic, less talkative and verbally expressive, less humorous, less imaginative, less unconventional, less lively and passionate, less perceptive, less apt to connect seemingly irrelevant things, less synthesizing, and less likely to see things from a different angle."[87]

Kim offers several explanations for the decline in creativity. The educational system has moved toward testing as a measure for success, encouraging children to study for the correct answer. Parents are encouraged to provide an activity-rich childhood for their kids, booking every free minute with classes, activities, and lessons. When children do have downtime, they tend to be over-supervised—and don't get much free time to explore, experiment, play, fail, and try again. Without the chance to be bored, it's difficult to be creative.

Adults who grew up with large chunks of unstructured time have an advantage—we know how valuable it can be to play. But we live in a goal-driven society. Productivity books and resources push scheduling every waking moment to get more done in less time. (Even this book offers tools to help you streamline your schedule.) In most of our social circles, talking about spending time daydreaming raises eyebrows and prompts derogatory comments. For many of us, our recreational time is also geared toward achievement, as we track and share our entertainment online.

So how can we address the problem of our dwindling imagination and creativity? We learn by doing. We need to practice imagining. No doubt, this creative play will support our writing. This quest has three tools to help you boost your imagination skills.

The Quest

Set aside time this week for creative play, and try one of the following tools to jump into the fun.

Play the "What If?" Game

As a chronic worrier, I play the "What If?" game all the time—what if my kids flunk out of school and have to live on my couch forever, what if that chicken I ate for lunch was bad, what if I never get this book published? Far better to play the "What if" fantasy game: what if squirrels were really super intelligent creatures and took over the world? (Yikes!) What if my library books talked to each other about who was reading them? What if the book I was reading spoke to me? What would it say?

Your assignment: Create 5-20 crazy "What if?" sentences. Then take one of them and follow it to its strangest conclusion.

Don't Look It Up, Make It Up!

Have you noticed how public wonderments have turned into competitive research sessions? You're standing in a park talking and someone says, "I wonder what people did for fun in Milwaukee in the mid-1800s?" Then five people pull out their smart phones and race to find out first. (Actually, the answer for that is easy, like the answer for all things Milwaukee: they drank beer.)

Your assignment: Write five questions that could require research. But don't touch your computer, smartphone, or tablet. Quickly make up 5-10 answers. If you've got time, develop one of them into a short story.

Invent It

When my dog had a giant sore on her ear (I know, yuck), we had quite a mess on our hands. It stunk and worse, every time she scratched, it bled all over the house. Before we brought her in to have the sore removed, I spent a lot of time devising ways to keep her from scratching it. (She can't use the Elizabethan collar.) Believe it or not, I had lots of fun trying to invent a protective ear device.

Your assignment: Invent a solution for a pesky problem in your house. If you don't have any problems (lucky you), get a bunch of stuff from your junk drawer and see what you can create with them.

Game Play Tips

- Play with these exercises until you find the one that works best for you.
- These tools can be helpful for brainstorming what comes next in your book. If you do use them for your creative work, keep generating ideas until you find a scenario that works for your book.
- Invite your allies (seen in "26. Identify Your Allies" on page 91) to join you in playing these problem-solving or imagination games.

For the Win

Imagining takes practice. In order to delve into imagining, you will need to let go of your need to get to the goal. But think of the fun you'll have playing with ideas!

74. IMPROVE YOUR WRITING

The marathon lifestyle promotes doing rather than watching…by adopting the marathon lifestyle you can confront your own lions, be your own hero, fight your own battles, challenge yourself.

– Richard Benyo

When I got out of bed Monday morning, I felt like I'd run a marathon or something. My leg muscles were sore, and I could barely lift my arms. I'd spent much of the weekend cleaning the house—squatting to dust baseboards, bending to retrieve dog toys, and running up and down the stairs to wash and put away the laundry. I exercise regularly. Why did my weekend cleaning spree hit me so hard?

In *Ten Things Trainers Wish You Knew about Your Workout*, trainer and fitness studio owner Michael Sokol said, "After doing the same cardio or strength routine three to six times, your body adapts and you burn fewer calories."[88] The article advised switching up routines. No wonder my body was so sore—my weekend chores challenged my muscles in a way my regular routine never did.

This got me thinking about writing. I wonder what happens to writers who consistently create in a single genre? Does churning out the same kind of copy day after day help us flourish or stifle our creativity? I don't think this is an either or dichotomy. Sticking with a genre or niche can help us learn it deeply and well. In time and with practice, we become better. But trying new things challenges our writing chops and can help us become better writers.

This quest provides five ways to challenge and stretch your writing muscles.

The Quest

Try one or all of the tools below and see how it impacts your writing.

Try a Contest

Tackling a writing contest can challenge us to sharpen our writing skills. Between undertaking a specific writing assignment and polishing up the piece for the judges, we work out our writing and revising muscles. *Prime Number Magazine* invites readers to write a 53-word short story based on a prompt. In the Your Story contest, *Writer's Digest* asks writers to compose a 650-word story based on a photo. And many magazines and foundations offer poetry and short story competitions.

Genre Jump

Maybe you're an expert at writing mysteries or nonfiction profiles. Imagine how you'll stretch your writing muscles if you try writing in a totally different genre. If you write primarily fiction, try nonfiction and vice versa. If you've already jumped genres, then think about playing with a new format. If you write novels, try flash fiction. If you write how-to books, take on an essay. Or try a new poem structure—a sonnet, a limerick, or an epic poem.

Take a Challenge

National Novel Writing Month was one of the best things to happen to the writing community because it turned writing a novel into a competitive sport. Of course, most people were competing with themselves and everyone could win—but still, it was a game changer. And now, the world is full of various writing challenges. Try Book in a Week, National Reading for Research Week, National Picture Book Writing Week, National Poetry Writing Month, or Script Race.

Take a Class

Maybe one of the best ways to level up our writing is to invite the information, guidance, and feedback of an experienced writing teacher. In a writing craft class, students can learn the specifics of a certain genre or dig into an aspect of writing—like crafting dialogue, orchestrating the plot, or creating voice. If you don't have access to an in-person class at a local college or writing center, try one of the many online writing communities.

Get Critiqued

Showing our writing to another person can be scary—especially when we're asking for critical feedback. But this practice can become a helpful tool in improving our writing. As first readers, our critique partners can help us see what's delightful and engaging about our work. They can also point out what doesn't work, noting both content and craft problems. Hearing their point of view can help us see our work in a new way. Find a partner or a group through writing organizations, local writing centers, or online writing educational sites.

Game Play Tips

- This quest takes courage! You'll be jumping into a brand new way of writing. But it also means that you'll grow as a writer.
- If you have another way to sharpen your writing practice—a class you've wanted to take, a book you've wanted to read, or a project you've hoped to take on—try it.
- Reflect on how changing up your writing practice improves your writing—and repeat as needed.

For the Win

We don't need to enroll in a MFA or a PhD program to level up our writing. This quest has taught us that when we learn a new technique, try a different genre, or get valuable feedback—we boost our skill level. Rock it, writers!

75. TRY STICKTOITIVENESS

The three great essentials to achieve anything worthwhile are, first, hard work; second, stick-to-itiveness; third, common sense.

— Thomas Edison

A few weeks ago, one of my brightest and most challenging students stayed after class to finish a project. Before he left he said, "You know, I hated this class at first. But I'm learning that if I focus on something, after a while I get into it. Now I like this class."

Wow.

I've had similar experiences with writing. I sometimes get projects that I really don't like or that seem too difficult. If I can make myself sit with the discomfort for a bit, then I sometimes have a breakthrough and get into the project. In those times, it can be hard to *stop* working.

In this quest, you'll work on sticking with a project or developing your *sticktoitiveness* and cultivating it as a habit.

The Quest

Next time you feel blocked or challenged by a project, don't give up. Instead, try brainstorming and writing with a timer to help you persist through the difficult parts. When you stick to a task through the difficult parts you can often find your way to the fun parts.

Set a Timer

Set aside 20-45 minutes to work on the project you feel stuck on. Use a timer to keep yourself on track.

Brainstorm

Instead of jumping right into writing something difficult, brainstorm. Use a mind map or list to gather ideas, possible directions, and solutions.

Write

When you hit on an idea that you feel energized by and want to write about, start writing.

Reward!

When the timer goes off, give yourself a reward for sticking to it! See the "Power-up List" on page 237 in the Appendix for ideas.

Repeat

One timed session might be all you need to get past that block and stick with a project. But if it isn't, don't fret. Set the timer and try again. In time, you'll blast past any blocks that you're experiencing and get into it!

Game Play Tips

- Review your ability to persist in other situations. Perhaps you're super persistent when it comes to overcoming conflict in relationships, creating meals out of bits and pieces, or enduring through a challenging exercise class. What skills from these experiences can you borrow to help you persist with writing?
- Try using your secret identity to help you persist through the tough parts. What are the strengths this part of your personality possesses that might help you?
- If you complete one timed writing session and still feel blocked, you may need to try a different tactic. Instead of writing, get away from the computer and do something fun. Take an adventure. Explore your local park. Read a book. Forget about your work for a bit and try again tomorrow. The break might just give you the aha moment you need. If you need more guidance, try the quests: "36. Move Your Body" on page 118, "58. Claim Idle Time" on page 181, or "72. Take a Scavenger Hunt" on page 217.

For the Win

Success happens to those who persist in the face of difficulty and failure. Keep going—and you'll get the boost and finish the book!

76. REFRAME REJECTION

To avoid criticism, say nothing, do nothing, be nothing.

– Aristotle

No one loves criticism, rejection, or failure. But if you're going to be a writer, you'll get a hefty dose of all three. Expecting it doesn't make it easier. Every time I encounter one of these roadblocks, I stumble. I want to eat chocolate, drink wine, and wallow in self-pity. And that's just fine— for a day. But a steady diet of self-pity won't help you move forward.

Many popular authors had their best books rejected multiple times. Publishers rejected my favorite childhood book, *A Wrinkle in Time* by Madeleine L'Engle, 26 times. British novelist Jasper Fforde accumulated 76 rejections before *The Eyre Affair* found a publisher. Two-time Newbery award winning author Kate DiCamillo received a whopping 473 rejections before her first book was published. But that's not all! James Baldwin, Ursula K. LeGuin, and Louisa May Alcott were all rejected! Imagine what our shelves would look like if these fine writers had given up? Pretty bare.

I remember attending a writing conference in California early in my career. A famous and much published writer began his talk by screaming at us: "No, no, no, no!" He then told us that we'd better get used to being turned down, because professional writers get rejected a lot. I don't know that I believed him. I'd heard too many fairy tales about the undiscovered writer getting plucked out of obscurity and offered a six-figure deal when an editor happened to hear her read at a writing conference. I wanted to believe the fairy tale.

Writers, I can tell you that the fairy tale is a lie. Look into the past of every good writer who appears to be an overnight success, and you will find messy first drafts and piles of rejection letters. The writers who get their stories, articles, and books published do so because they worked hard and didn't let a tiny little thing like a rejection letter stop them.

In this quest, you will create a plan to reframe rejection and keep moving forward.

The Quest

Don't ever see a rejection from a job, a submission, or a person as a stop sign from the universe. Instead, let it remind you that you are a working writer. Use this quest to deal with any rejection you receive.

Step One: Look for Information

When we treat a rejection letter as information instead of a judgment, we can use that information to move forward. Does the rejection letter have anything to teach you about your work? Is there a reason the submission didn't work for this agent or editor?

Step Two: Consider Next Steps

Use the information you gained from the rejection letter to think about your next steps. Ask questions like:

- Do you need to revise the work to make it more sellable?
- Do you need to revise your pitch for your work, to help agents or editors understand it more fully?
- Would the piece be better suited to another agent or editor?
- Could you do something different with the piece—perhaps indie publish it?
- Where will you send it next?

Step Three: Move Forward

If you know your next step for this project, then take it. If you don't know what to do next, dig into a new project. Spend a little time each week working on a new story or project that gives you energy and joy.

Game Play Tips

- Prepare to repeat this quest a lot—writers get rejected. If you need more help dealing with rejection, try the quest "49. Explain Well" on page 156.
- Next time you experience rejection, ask: what's next? Then do it. Take one step forward. Just one. Send out a query letter, write a blog post, or sign up for a writing class. Do anything to stay in the game.
- Get support! Connect with your allies (over in "26. Identify Your Allies" on page 91)—especially other writers and creatives who have experienced rejection—and hear how they turned it around and kept writing. Their stories will help you reframe your own rejection.

For the Win

In time, the sting that comes with criticism, rejection, or failure will fade. You'll be able to treat the rejection as information and move forward, toward success.

77. WRITE FIFTEEN MINUTES A DAY

If I have ten minutes I use them even if they bring only two lines, and it keeps the book alive.

– Rumer Godden

So how do you write when you have no time? That's not a stupid question. We all encounter periods when we have no time to write. And those who work full time or are new to writing may find it more challenging to squeeze in writing time. How do we write when we have no time, money, energy, or clean laundry? How do we find five minutes to string together words when we don't want to get up earlier, stay up later, give up our lunch hour or coffee break, or take a weekend to write? At times, between managing work, home, family, and friends, it's all we can do to eat and find clean underwear.

On her blog, author Laurie Halse Anderson challenged writers to write fifteen minutes a day (WFMAD). That's it. There were no additional rules, no word count goals, no projects to complete—just write for fifteen minutes every single day.

When life gets busy, even fifteen minutes can seem like a lot of time. In this quest, you'll try out multiple ways of writing for fifteen minutes a day. At the end of the quest, you'll have a better idea of how to squeeze in writing time!

The Quest
For the next week, try to squeeze in chunks of 15-minute writing sessions. Try one or more of the ideas below to discover how and when it's best for you to write.

First Thing
Write first thing in the morning, before you get out of bed. Before you are fully conscious just grab pen and paper and write for fifteen minutes. (Yes, you may have to set your alarm fifteen or twenty minutes early.)

Last Thing
Turn in early and write for fifteen minutes before you go to sleep. Instead of depending on your favorite authors to tell you a bedtime story, tell yourself a bedtime story. Just get those thoughts down on paper.

Waiting Time
Write while you're waiting in the car to pick up your children from school, soccer practice, or a play date. If you don't have children, write anytime

you are forced to wait—perhaps while waiting for your conference call to get started or the coffee to brew. You may not get fifteen minutes all at once, but you will be writing more than you do now.

Email Time

When you open email, before you read or answer even one message, write the first email to yourself. Take fifteen minutes and write your chunk in an email—or just pretend you're writing in an email and put it in a regular document.

Social Media Time

If you're at all like most of us, much of the time we spend on social media moves from productive to mindless fairly quickly. Why not take back *that* time for something meaningful to you? Before you wander over to Facebook for the fifth time today to look through all of your friends' happy status updates or check out the posts on Instagram or Twitter, write your chunk. Take fifteen minutes of the time you are currently using for social media and write.

Coffee Time

Tie your writing to something else you already do every day—like your morning coffee break. If you don't take a coffee break, write during the first half of your lunch hour. Write while you are on the bus or train to work. Devote fifteen minutes to writing before you allow yourself to catch up with the *Real Housewives* of wherever.

Game Play Tips

- It's hard to break our habits, especially automatic habits like emailing, texting, and surfing. For this tool to work, you may need to find a way to interrupt that habit and write first. Put a sticky note reminder on the computer (real or virtual), set an alarm on your phone, or ask a friend to send you a Facebook message encouraging you to write. No matter what happens, keep trying. You'll get better at honoring your writing time, and the words will add up!
- Be prepared for failure. This quest offers multiple ways to squeeze in short bursts of writing because not all of them will work for you. Be sure to try at least three of the above ideas—or invent your own.
- If your fifteen minutes happens to be while you're away from home, don't worry. Write or dictate into your phone's notes app, email yourself, or record your chunk. Of course, writing in a notebook or on the back of an envelope works well, too.

For the Win

When the quest is over, you'll have a new writing habit. Imagine that! You may also have amassed a bunch more words. Yay you!

78. WAIT PRODUCTIVELY

We haven't remained idle, twiddling our thumbs while you were off having a good time.

— V.C. Andrews

We rarely expect to wait. Oh, it happens all the time, but we don't expect it. And because we don't expect it, we're often not prepared for it.

Several years ago, I took a trip to Texas to meet with coaching clients. I expected a fairly easy travel day, hopping on the plane just after 11:00 AM and arriving in Texas at 2:00 PM. Shortly after getting on the plane, the captain told us that there was a slight delay because they had to jumpstart the plane. That wasn't something I needed to hear. More time passed, the captain informed us that we were waiting for a nonessential part that we should have, just in case. Just in case of what?

We waited longer, and the cabin grew hotter. Finally, the captain let us off the plane. We waited for another two hours at the gate. We boarded the plane again at 3:00 PM, waiting another hour for the plane to get weighed. Finally at 4:00 PM, five hours after we'd first boarded the plane, we took off.

I'd dropped my daughter off at school before leaving for the airport. When she came home from school, we talked again. I was still at my home airport. She had attended a full day of school, including a field trip to see a play, while I had spent the day waiting. During that long delay, I read books, played games on my iPod, read a magazine, talked to my family, listened in on other conversations, texted my colleagues, and snacked. I did not do what I would encourage other writers to do: write. Instead, I let the distractions of the airport and worries about arriving on time rule my day. Never again. Next time I get in this situation—and you know there will be a next time—I want to be prepared.

In this quest, you'll create a plan to make waiting time work for you.

The Quest

Step One: Choose a Path
Consider and list all the ways you might use waiting time. Here are some ideas:

Working. Reading documents, writing pitches, writing stories, composing articles, or editing.

Connecting. Connect with friends and colleagues on the phone or through social media.

Reading. Listen to or read information from podcasts, books, magazines, and blogs.

Collecting Ideas and Impressions. Waiting can be a great time to learn from those around us and collect ideas for stories or characters.

Journaling. Use your extra time to do those writing exercises you never have time for.

Spiritual Practice. You may not be able to meditate while waiting in line for your favorite ride at Disney World, but you may be able to practice deep breathing, balance on one foot, or repeat a mantra.

Step Two: Create a Waiting Toolbox

Thanks to smartphones and tablets, all of us have a wealth of information and tools that we can use when we are waiting. Here are some ways to transform your smartphone or tablet into your work cubicle or retreat tool while you wait.

- Keep a writing assignment or a list of writing tasks with you at all times. Use Google Docs, Evernote, or another online project management tool.
- Get a word processing app for your smart phone or tablet or use a note-taking app to write while you're away from home.
- Load up your phone or tablet with podcasts, music, and other audio material. In addition, download an app that allows you to borrow audiobooks from your local public library.
- Use a reading app to put books on your phone or tablet.
- Use an app like Evernote or Pocket to save important articles.

Step Three: Practice!

Try out some of your waiting tasks in the next week—and reflect on what works best for you. Be patient, as it may take time to figure out that some tasks work better in specific places. For example, it might be difficult to write a report for work when sitting with your children in a busy pediatric waiting room. But it might be the perfect place to collect ideas.

Game Play Tips

- Make technology work for you. If you're waiting in a noisy place, use your MP3 player to listen to music or white noise while you work.
- Make a game of it. How many words can you write during a layover? Try to improve your word count each time you wait.
- Find inspiration. If you forget to do any of the above things, don't despair. Watch people and listen in on conversations. All of these experiences will be fodder for stories.

For the Win

Since smartphones and tablets have become a ubiquitous tool, we hardly need to worry about waiting anymore. Everyone can pass time by checking up on their social media feeds. Hopefully, this quest has helped you find productive ways to make waiting work for you.

APPENDIX

POWER-UP LIST

In a running marathon, you hit the wall when you deplete all of the glycogen stored in the liver and muscles. When you play video games, you lose a life when you run out of health points. Similarly, if you write and vision regularly, you'll deplete your creative energy.

Criticism, rejection, and inner doubt can also damage our resolve to write. It depletes our inner reserves. In *Daybook*, Anne Truitt wrote about harsh critiques of her *Arundel* exhibit at the Baltimore Museum of Art. She said, "I am not concerned with reviewers' judgments, yea or nay; they cannot deflect my course. What they can do, and this seems beyond my resistance, is hurt my general self, the supporting troops, so to speak, of my striking force."[89]

In video game terminology, power-ups provide boosts of energy, strength, or special powers for the player. In life, power-ups are any activity that makes "you feel happier, stronger, healthier or better connected."[90] This is a list of power-ups that can help you strengthen your soul in the midst of criticism and doubt. Star the ones that work for you. Then make a list of ten soul-strengthening actions and do them regularly. When you're feeling especially low, give yourself a day of nurture! (Check out "58. Claim Idle Time" on page 181 and "59. Take an Inspiration Sabbatical" on page 183 for suggestions on taking time off.)

Artist's Date

In *The Artist's Way*, Julia Cameron encourages readers to take a weekly artist's date to nourish their creativity. As Cameron says in her follow-up book, *Walking in This World*, "Always, when I return to the practice of Artist's Dates, my sense of well-being increases and my work deepens and enlarges."[91] Take yourself on an artist's date. You might visit a fabric store, sketch in the park, or wander through an art gallery.

Art Making

Making art can be extremely healing. Studies show that it improves well-being by decreasing negative emotions and increasing positive ones, improves flow and spontaneity, and improves medical outcomes.[92] Get art supplies and play! Use watercolor paints to capture the blooms on your winter cactus or try creating a collage.

You can supercharge this power-up by making art with others. Socializing carries additional benefits: it strengthens the immune system, increases one's sense of well-being, and supports brain health. There are several ways to make art with friends. Gather a group of friends and invite one of them to bring a craft to teach the group. Or hire a local artist to lead you and your friends in an art experience. If you live in an area with an art bar or public classes, you can take a class together.

Baby Animals!

Researchers have discovered that looking at photos of cute baby animals can increase our focus and help us to get more writing done.[93] If you don't have a kitten or duckling handy, find one of the many sites filled with baby animal pictures and videos and check it out next time you need a lift.

Chop Wood, Carry Water

When Michael Gelb, author of *How to Think Like Leonardo DaVinci*, asked creatives where they got their best ideas, their most popular answers were: in the shower, while walking in nature, listening to music, or napping. Greek polymath Archimedes got the very first Eureka moment while in the public bath. Herbert Benson, in his book *The Breakout Principle*, suggests that we can overcome our mental blocks by walking away from our work and doing something that is both mindless and repetitive, such as knitting, folding towels, or chopping wood. While you're working on the mindless task—or napping or bathing—your subconscious is hard at work solving your problem. At some point, you land on the exact solution you need—the aha moment you've been searching for.

Colorful Mood Boosters

Do you look at a photo of a deep blue lake and instantly feel calmer? Or see an expansive field of green and experience a wave of peace? Or maybe you've noticed that just looking at a red can of soda energizes you. Research has shown that colors affect our memory, arouse our emotions, and can boost our energy. Green improves concentration, orange lifts moods and increases critical thinking skills, blue stimulates creativity and boosts productivity, and pink can calm us. Play with using color to support your writing productivity. Wear it, decorate with it, or simply create a Pinterest board for your favorite brain boosting colors!

Coloring Calm

Carl Jung encouraged his patients to create and color mandalas, using the objects as tools for helping him diagnose his patients. Today, art therapists and ordinary people use coloring to calm anxiety, boost mindfulness, and increase focus. A 2005 research study showed that coloring mandalas reduced anxiety.[94]

For years, I've practiced making and coloring mandalas with my family. I use *Everyone's Mandala Coloring Book* by Monique Mandali as my grown up coloring book. In my house, this is usually a family activity. We take out the colored pencils, put on music, and color. Not only is the practice relaxing, I usually come up with a few writing ideas when I color. If you're an adventurous sort, try making your own mandala and then coloring it! If you really love coloring, purchase one of the many new adult coloring books available or try a coloring app for your tablet.

Connect

As mentioned in *Art Making* above, connecting with others brings many physical and mental benefits. Socializing speeds healing, lowers levels of anxiety and depression, increases self-esteem, improves our ability to empathize, and may even lead to a longer life. Isolating ourselves carries great risks, and in one study researchers found loneliness to be as detrimental to our health as obesity, smoking, and high blood pressure.[95] Of course, who we connect with matters. Great writers surround themselves with people who are smart, imaginative, and visionary. Austin Kleon, author of *Steal Like an Artist*, encourages creatives to build idea incomes by connecting with brilliant people. That means, say no to any committee meeting or connecting with duds and complainers.

Dim the Lights

Do you feel more creative during the shortest days of the year? There may be a reason for that. In one study, participants who worked in dim lighting were better able to generate innovative ideas. German researchers Anna Steidle and Lioba Werth explained that dim light, "elicits a feeling of freedom, self-determination, and reduced inhibition."[96]

Doodle

One of my wonderful clients introduced me to Zentangle, the art of meditative doodling. I bought a book, *Totally Tangled* by Sandra Bartholomew, a pen, and started doodling. It's one of my favorite ways to take a break and get inspired. The cartoonist Charles Barsotti takes a big stack of paper and doodles until the "aha moment" occurs.

Drink Water

We know that we need to drink water to stay healthy. But did you know that drinking water can improve your mood? When we drink water, even if we're not super thirsty, we feel refreshed. One study showed that students who brought water to an exam got better grades.[97] While many writers use alcohol to fuel their creativity—think of William Faulkner's ready bottle of whiskey or Patricia Highsmith's gin—water might work better, and keep you clear enough to keep writing!

Flower Power

Can flowers boost your energy? According to a Harvard study, people who saw fresh blooms in the morning reported an increase in energy levels for the entire day.[98] I wonder if that's why my great aunt Alma, who lived in Northern Minnesota, kept a table in her living room filled with blooming African violets. Grow flowers in a pot on your front porch or in your office. In the winter, try growing a Christmas Cactus or an indoor bulb. Or simply pick up flowers from the grocery store or farmer's market.

Gratitude Journal

Professor Robert Emmons and his colleague Professor Mike McCullough have conducted many gratitude studies. Gratitude has a powerful effect. It boosts the dopamine in our brain, just like the antidepressant Wellbutrin. It also boosts serotonin production in the brain, just like Prozac.[99] Part of the research suggests that even just looking for things to be grateful for is helpful.

Each evening, record three blessings from the day. Or, give yourself a scavenger hunt in the morning—challenge yourself to look for three acts of kindness, three signs of love, or three unusual pieces of art. You'll be surprised at how that small act of intention will help you see more throughout your day. In the evening, record your discoveries.

Learn!

When we learn something new, it boosts our energy. When we learn a skill that requires us to continually access our long-term memory and challenges us to keep solving problems, then we are also building brain function.[100] Talk about a power-up! This kind of activity is called productive engagement, and just doing a crossword puzzle won't engage us enough. Take a break to learn a photo-editing tool, a new language, or a musical instrument—you'll feel energized and your brain will, too!

Meditate

Meditation benefits us in many ways. It reduces stress, controls anxiety, improves our ability to focus, improves sleep, and promotes emotional health. Start with five minutes of attending to your breathing. From there, let your practice grow in time and quality. If silence isn't your thing, try a guided meditation. If you have difficulty sitting for a long period of time, try a walking meditation.

Messy Creativity

The stacks of paper in your office or piles of dishes in your kitchen might help you be more inventive. In a study led by Kathleen D. Vohs of the University of Minnesota, Carlson School of Management, researchers put participants in either a messy or a neat office space and asked them to imagine novel uses for Ping-Pong balls. Both groups of subjects came up with about the same number of answers, but the participants who worked in the messy room developed "almost five times the number of highly-creative responses" as the others.[101] Try working in a messy space—or create a mess as you work. See if the messy environment makes you more or less inventive.

Music Boost

We all know that a road trip is more fun with a great soundtrack, but do you know why? Listening to music makes people happier! Research by the University of Missouri shows that listening to upbeat music can immediately lift our mood and, over a two-week period of regular listening, increase our general feelings of well-being.[102] Some writers create a playlist for each project, while others save music for the breaks between writing sessions. I've found that attending concerts provides an additional boost in mood and energy because I get to appreciate music with other people.

Nap

Take a nap. Short naps can help you restore your ability to pay attention and get work done. In a Harvard study, subjects whose performance on tasks had dropped by as much as 50 percent throughout the day took a one-hour nap and completely restored their highest levels of performance.[103] New research also promotes the effectiveness of a coffee nap. Participants who drank 2 cups of coffee then took a 20-minute nap increased their energy levels and felt more alert. Researchers say this works because the nap helps the body absorb the caffeine. Of course, if you don't want to disrupt your sleep, it's good to practice the coffee nap at least six hours before bedtime.[104]

Reward Yourself

One way to keep your butt in the chair is to promise yourself a reward. Famous writers have rewarded themselves in unique ways: Anthony Burgess used the Martini Method, relaxing with a dry martini at the end of each day. I suggest more healthy rewards. A walk in the park. An hour reading a good book. A trip to the library. Healthy rewards at the end of a day of writing will remind you that writing has its rewards—and you'll be much more likely to get your butt in the chair next time!

Savor Joy

When we remember our happiest moments, we feel happier now. Researcher Fred Bryant found that people who looked at pictures of happy times in their lives felt happier in the present moment.[105] Take a look through your phone's photos and find an experience that brought you joy. It can be something small, like noticing the perfect blue sky or spending an hour having coffee with a friend. Take a moment to remember the details and bask in the moment. If you don't have enough photos on your phone, make a list of happy past events. They can be big events, like a family holiday party, or smaller ones like watching a neighborhood child eat an ice cream cone on a hot day. Recall the experience in vivid detail, like playing a movie in your mind, or write about it in your journal.

Sing

If you watched *Sesame Street* as a child, you may have heard Joe Raposo's famous song, "Sing," encouraging listeners to sing along, whether they were good singers or not! And for good reason—singing alone and with others has all sorts of benefits. Singing is a workout, strengthening our diaphragm, improving our breathing and circulation. One study even found that singing improved the immune system of the singers. And if that's not enough to get you to sing along, listen to this: Scientists believe that when we sing with a group, it lowers our stress levels, decreases anxiety, and increases endorphins. And according to a 2005 study, you don't have to be good at singing to get these benefits.[106] So sing: in the shower, on the street, or in a choir!

Stair Climbing

When you're stuck, tired, and tempted to grab a soda, try taking the stairs. In a 2017 study published in the journal *Physiology and Behavior*, researchers from the UGA College of Education discovered that just 10 minutes of walking up and down the stairs was more likely to energize participants than taking in 50 milligrams of caffeine, about what one finds in a can of soda.[107] Wowza—stairs here we come!

Vacation!

Professor Fred Bryant, author of *Thanks! How Practicing Gratitude Can Make You Happier*, encourages people to try the 20-minute vacation exercise.[108] Carve out 20 minutes a day to do something you love, perhaps gardening, beading, building, painting—anything that brings you joy. Dedicate that 20 minutes to your activity—don't try to work or check on social media or anything else during that time. Notice how you feel and what you enjoy. At the end of your vacation, intentionally plan the next day's vacation and anticipate it. At the end of the day look back on your vacation and savor it.

If planning a daily vacation is too challenging, create a writing rest stop in your house. Stock it with fun magazines and tasty snacks. Whenever you feel overwhelmed, take a 20-minute break and visit the rest stop. Sip a cool drink and read about how to organize your spice drawer or what to do in Cancun, Mexico. When you feel less frantic and more focused, return to writing.

Walk!

Moderate physical activity can increase cognitive capacity—by driving more blood and oxygen to the brain. In *Write-A-Thon*, I wrote about a study that showed that women who walked had better brain connectivity.[109]

But that's not all! While at Stanford University's Graduate School of Education, Marily Oppezzo, PhD, and colleague Daniel L. Schwartz, PhD, did a number of studies that found students who walked performed better on tests that measure creativity, especially free-flowing thoughts. They did less well on tests that required a single answer.[110]

And another study by Marc G. Berman, John Jonides, and Stephen Kaplan at the University of Michigan found that walking in nature can restore our ability to pay attention, something that usually diminishes throughout the day.[111] But if you don't live near the wilderness, don't worry. Just go outside. Take a walk in the park. Dig in your garden. Watch the birds or the bugs.

The "You Rock" Journal

Several years ago, I purchased a journal and filled it with love letters and sweet quotes for my husband. It made a great Christmas gift that he held onto over the years. Find a journal you like (or make your own out of an old book) and fill it with:

- Inspiring writing and reading quotes
- Quotes from your favorite books
- Encouraging notes from readers, editors, and friends
- Lists of your achievements
- Lists of your strengths

ENDNOTES

1   David Bayles and Ted Orland, *Art and Fear: Observations on the Perils (and Rewards) of Artmaking* (Santa Cruz, CA: The Image Continuum, 1993), 35-36.

2   Edward Packard, *You Are a Genius* (New York: Bantam Press, 1989).

3   Jane McGonigal, *SuperBetter: A Revolutionary Approach to Getting Stronger, Happier, Braver, and More Resilient* (New York: Penguin Press, 2015), 1.

4   Sheldon, K. M., & Lyubomirsky, S. (2006). "How to increase and sustain positive emotion: the effects of expressing gratitude and visualizing best possible selves." *Journal of Positive Psychology*, 1, 73-82.

5   Martha Beck, "Getting Rid of Stuff," *Martha Beck Blog*, August 2012, https://marthabeck.com/2012/08/getting-rid-of-stuff/

6   In the article, Martha Beck refers to this as her, Pray Rain Journal, a concept developed by Jeannette Maw and written about in her book: *The Magic of Pray Rain Journaling*. (Self-published, Amazon Digital Services, 2011), Kindle.

7   Gretchen Rubin, "My Best Advice for Graduates: 12 Tips for A Happy Life," *Gretchen Rubin* (blog), May 23, 2017, https://gretchenrubin.com/2017/05/advice-for-graduates-tips-happy-life/

8   North, A. C., Hargreaves, D. J., & McKendrick, J. (1999). "The influence of in-store music on wine selections." *Journal of Applied Psychology*, 84 (2), 271-276.

9   Ralph Fletcher, *A Writer's Notebook: Unlocking the Writer Within You* (New York: HarperTrophy, 1996).

10 Luther Snow, *The Power of Asset Mapping: How Your Congregation Can Act on Its Gifts* (Lanham, MD: Roman and Littlefield, 2004).

11 Brené Brown, *The Gifts of Imperfection: Let Go of Who You Think You're Supposed to Be and Embrace Who You Are*, (Center City, MN: Hazelden, 2010), 56-57.

12 Cheryl Richardson, *Take Time for Your Life: A Personal Coach's 7-Step Program for Creating the Life You Want* (New York: Broadway Books, 1999).

13 Rochelle Melander, *Write-A-Thon: Write Your Book in 26 Days (And Live to Tell About It)* (Cincinnati: Writer's Digest, 2011).

14 Anne Lamott, *Operating Instructions: A Journal of My Son's First Year* (New York: Ballantine Books, 1994), 48-9.

15 Gil Rendle and Alice Mann, *Holy Conversations: Strategic Planning as Spiritual Practice for Congregations* (Lanham, MD: Roman and Littlefield, 2004).

16 Ellyn Spragin, *What I Know Now: Letters to My Younger Self*. (New York: Harmony, 2006).

17 Stephen Battaglio, "The Biz: Norman Lear Shares His Life Lessons," *TV Guide*, October 27-Nov. 9, 2014, 7.

18 Nelson, Leif D., and Michael I. Norton. "From Student to Superhero: Situational Primes Shape Future Helping," *Journal of Experimental Social Psychology* 41, no. 4 (July 2005): 423–430.

19   Jane McGonigal, *SuperBetter: A Revolutionary Approach to Getting Stronger, Happier, Braver, and More Resilient* (New York: Penguin Press, 2015), 101.

20   Nelson, Leif D., and Michael I. Norton. "From Student to Superhero: Situational Primes Shape Future Helping," *Journal of Experimental Social Psychology* 41, no. 4 (July 2005): 426.

21   Sue Shellenbarger, "The Peak Time for Everything," *The Wall Street Journal* (online), posted September 26, 2012

22   "A Writer's Room," *T Magazine*, August 25, 2013.

23   Jane McGonigal, *SuperBetter: A Revolutionary Approach to Getting Stronger, Happier, Braver, and More Resilient* (New York: Penguin Press, 2015), 160.

24   Chris Weller, "A neuroscientist who studies decision-making reveals the most important choice you can make," *Business Insider* (online), July 28, 2017.

25   Weller, *Business Insider*.

26   Gail M. Sullivan, "So You Want to Write? Practices that Work," *Journal of Graduate Medical Education*. 2013 Sep; 5(3): 357–359.

27   Flannery O'Connor, *The Habit of Being: Letters of Flannery O'Connor* (New York: Farrar, Straus, and Giroux, 1988).

28   Charles Duhigg, *The Power of Habit: Why We Do What We Do in Life and Business* (New York: Random House, 2012).

29   Robert Maurer, *One Small Step Can Change Your Life: The Kaizen Way* (New York: Workman Publishing, 2004).

30   Many of these tools are also discussed in the introduction.

31   John Tierney, "Do You Suffer from Decision Fatigue," *New York Times Magazine*, August 17, 2011, https://www.nytimes.com/2011/08/21/magazine/do-you-suffer-from-decision-fatigue.html.

32   Dr. Michael F. Roizen and Dr. Mehmet Oz, *You: On a Diet* (New York: Scribner, 2009).

33   Joshua Becker, "21 Surprising Statistics that Reveal How Much Stuff We Actually Own," *Becoming Minimalist* (blog), https://www.becomingminimalist.com/clutter-stats/.

34   Edward Hallowell, "Overloaded Circuits: Why Smart People Underperform," *Harvard Business Review*, 2005.

35   Virginia Woolf, *The Diary of Virginia Woolf: Volume One 1915-1919* (New York: HBJ, 1977), 266.

36   David Sedaris, "Ask the Author Live: David Sedaris," *The New Yorker*, August 14, 2009, https://www.newyorker.com/books/ask-the-author/ask-the-author-live-david-sedaris.

37   Elizabeth George, *Write Away: One Novelists Approach to Fiction and the Writing Life*, (New York: Harper Perennial, 2005), 199.

38   Tara Parker-Pope, "Workplace cited as a New Source in Rise of Obesity," *New York Times* (online), May 26, 2011, https://www.nytimes.com/2011/05/26/health/nutrition/26fat.html

39   John Green, *Turtles All The Way Down*, (New York: Dutton, 2017), 7.

40   Vaish, A., Grossmann, T., & Woodward, A. (2008). Not all emotions are created equal: The negativity bias in social-emotional development. *Psychological Bulletin*, 134 (3), 383-403.

41   Duckworth, Angela & Kirby, Teri & Oettingen, Gabriele & Gollwitzer, Anton, "From Fantasy to Action: Mental Contrasting With Implementation Intentions (MCII) Improves Academic Performance in Children." *Social Psychological and Personality Science*, 2013 Nov 1; 4(6): 745–753, https://doi.org/10.1177/1948550613476307

42   Matt McWiliams, "Four Types of Limiting Beliefs that Cripple Your Growth," blog, https://www.mattmcwilliams.com/4-types-limiting-beliefs-cripple-growth/.

43   Byron Katie, *Loving What Is: Four questions that can change your life* (New York: Three Rivers Press, 2002), 26.

44   Katie, *Loving What Is*, p, 96.

45   Pema Chödrön, "How Lojong Awakens Your Heart," *Lion's Roar* (online), November 22, 2017, https://www.lionsroar.com/dont-give-up/.

46   M. J. Ryan, *Habit Changers: 82 Game-Changing Mantras to Mindfully Realize Your Goals*, (New York: Crown Business, 2016), 5.

47   Paul Hammerness, M.D., Margaret Moore, and John Hane, *Organize Your Mind, Organize Your Life: Train Your Brain to Get More Done in Less Time*, (New York: Harlequin, 2011).

48   Jill Bolte Taylor, *My Stroke of Insight: A Brain Scientist's Personal Journey* (New York: A Plume Book, 2006), 153.

49   Brent Crane, "For a More Creative Brain, Travel," *The Atlantic*, March 31, 2015, https://www.theatlantic.com/health/archive/2015/03/for-a-more-creative-brain-travel/388135/.

50   Belle Beth Cooper, "The Secret to Creativity, Intelligence, and Scientific Thinking," *Buffer* (blog), January 22, 2014, https://buffer.com/resources/connections-in-the-brain-understanding-creativity-and-intelligenceconnections.

51   Belle Beth Cooper, "Why Getting New Things Makes Us Feel So Good: Novelty and the Brain," *LifeHacker* (blog), May 21, 2013, https://lifehacker.com/novelty-and-the-brain-why-new-things-make-us-feel-so-g-508983802.

52   Denise C. Park, Jennifer Lodi-Smith, Linda Drew, Sara Haber, Andrew Hebrank, Gérard N. Bischof, Whitley Aamodt, "The Impact of Sustained Engagement on Cognitive Function," (January, 2014), *Psychological Science*, Volume: 25 issue: 1, page(s): 103-112, https://doi.org/10.1177/0956797613499592.

53   Jacque Wilson, "This is Your Brain on Crafting," *CNN*, January 5, 2015, https://www.cnn.com/2014/03/25/health/brain-crafting-benefits/.

54   Brent Crane, "For a More Creative Brain, Travel: How international experiences can open the mind to new ways of thinking," *The Atlantic*, March 31, 2015, https://www.theatlantic.com/health/archive/2015/03/for-a-more-creative-brain-travel/388135/.

55   Christopher Bergland, "Want to Improve Your Cognitive Abilities? Go Climb a Tree!," *Psychology Today* (blog), July 30, 2015, https://www.psychologytoday.com/us/blog/the-athletes-way/201507/want-improve-your-cognitive-abilities-go-climb-tree.

56   Oppezzo, M., & Schwartz, D. L. (2014). "Give your ideas some legs: The positive effect of walking on creative thinking," *Journal of Experimental Psychology: Learning, Memory, and Cognition*, 40 (4), 1142-1152.

57   KI Erickson, MW Voss, RS Prakash, C Basak, A Szabo, L Chaddock, "Exercise training increases size of hippocampus and improves memory," *Proceedings of the National Academy of Sciences*, 108 (7), 3017-3022.

58   Bill Burnett and Dave Evans, *Designing Your Life: How to Build a Well-Lived, Joyful Life*, (New York: Knopf, 2016), 66.

59   The introduction presents information on how to mind map.

60   Elizabeth Lombardo, *Better Than Perfect: 7 Strategies to Crush Your Inner Critic and Create a Life You Love* (Berkeley, CA: Seal Press, 2014), 65.

61   Bob Sullivan and Hugh Thompson, *The Plateau Effect: Getting from Stuck to Success* (New York: Dutton, 2013), 165.

62   Bob Sullivan and Hugh Thompson, *The Plateau Effect*, 165.

63   Chris Gayomali, "Small Distractions Are Making You A Terrible Writers, Says Science," *Fast Company* (Online), July 7, 2014, https://www.fastcompany.com/3033189/small-distractions-are-making-you-a-terrible-writer-says-science.

64   "Brief Interruptions Spawn Errors," *MSU Today*, January 7, 2013, https://msutoday.msu.edu/news/2013/brief-interruptions-spawn-errors/.

65   "Mutltitasking hurts performance but makes you feel better," *Science Daily*, April 30, 2012.

66   Will Knight, "Info-Mania Dents IQ More Than Marijuana," *New Scientist Daily News*, April 22, 2005, https://www.newscientist.com/article/dn7298-info-mania-dents-iq-more-than-marijuana/.

67   "Apply the brakes" is a phrase used in the book, *Organize Your Mind, Organize Your Life: Train Your Brain to Get More Done in Less Time*, by Paul Hammerness, M.D., Margaret Moore, and John Hane, (New York: Harlequin, 2011), 95-118.

68   Patricia Ryan Madson, *Improv Wisdom: Don't Prepare, Just Show Up.* (New York: Bell Tower, 2005), 86.

69   Mark Murphy, "The Way You Check Email Is Making You Less Productive," *Forbes*, September 18, 2016, https://www.forbes.com/sites/markmurphy/2016/09/18/the-way-you-check-email-is-making-you-less-productive/#6fb989b937e3

70   Lisa Eadicicco, "Americans Check their Phones 8 Billion Times A Day," *Time*, December 15, 2015, http://time.com/4147614/smartphone-usage-us-2015/.

71   "How Much Time Do People Spend on Their Mobile Phones in 2017?," *Hackernoon* (blog), May 9, 2017, https://hackernoon.com/how-much-time-do-people-spend-on-their-mobile-phones-in-2017-e5f90a0b10a6.

72   David DiSalvo, "Study: Engaging with Social Media Can Drain Your Brain," *Psychology Today* (blogs), June 1, 2016, https://www.psychologytoday.com/us/blog/neuronarrative/201606/study-engaging-social-media-can-drain-your-brain.

73   Will Knight, "Info-Mania Dents IQ More Than Marijuana," *New Scientist Daily News*, April 22, 2005, https://www.newscientist.com/article/dn7298-info-mania-dents-iq-more-than-marijuana/.

74   Sharon Gaudin, "Americans Spend 16 Minutes of Every Hour Online on Social Nets," *Computer World*, April 17, 2013, https://www.computerworld.

com/article/2496852/americans-spend-16-minutes-of-every-hour-online-on-social-nets.html.

75   Kalina Christoff, Alan M. Gordon, Jonathan Smallwood, Rachelle Smith, and Jonathan W. Schooler, "Experience sampling during fMRI reveals default network and executive system contributions to mind wandering," *Proceedings of the National Academy of Sciences*, 2009, https://doi.org/10.1073/pnas.0900234106.

76   Michael Vaughn, "Know Your Limits, Your Brain Can Only Take So Much," *Entrepreneur*, January 21, 2014, https://www.entrepreneur.com/article/230925.

77   Paul Hammerness, M.D., Margaret Moore, and John Hane, *Organize Your Mind, Organize Your Life: Train Your Brain to Get More Done in Less Time*, (New York: Harlequin, 2011).

78   USA Today Snapshots, *USA Today Weekend Edition*, August 10-12, 2012.

79   Sebastian Bailey and Octavius Black, *Mind Gym: Achieve More By Thinking Differently* (New York: HarperOne, 2014).

80   Tony Schwartz and Jim Loehr, *The Power of Full Engagement: Managing Energy, Not Time, Is the Key to High Performance and Personal Renewal* (New York: Free Press, 2003).

81   Ernest Hemingway, "Monologue to the Maestro: A High Seas Letter," *Esquire*, October 1935.

82   "Planning Fallacy," Wikipedia, last modified February 2, 2019, https://en.wikipedia.org/wiki/Planning_fallacy.

83   "Planning Fallacy," Wikipedia.

84   John Morse, https://www.kailinart.com/john-morse/

85   Here are some resources that may help you to play with poetry.
      Poems to Learn By Heart edited by Caroline Kennedy. I picked up this delightful collection of children's poetry at the library. Even if you don't have a child in your life, read it aloud!
      Dancing with Joy: 99 Poems edited by Roger Housden. This collection of poems from 69 poets offers a rich vision of what it means to experience joy.
      Haiku Mind: 108 Poems to Cultivate Awareness & Open Your Heart by Patricia Donegan. If you can't focus on a long poem, try reading haiku. These short, pithy poems help readers practice mindfulness. In this collection, Donegan reflects on each poem and provides a biography of the author.

86   Lewis Carroll, *Alice's Adventures in Wonderland*, (Mineola, NY: Dover Thrift Editions, 1993), 1-2.

87   Peter Gray, "As Children's Freedom Has Declined, So Has Their Creativity," *The Creativity Post*, September 29, 2012, http://www.creativitypost.com/education/as_childrens_freedom_has_declined_so_has_their_creativity.

88   Karen Asp, "10 Things Trainers Wish You Knew About Your Workout," *Real Simple*, January 2012, https://www.realsimple.com/health/fitness-exercise/things-trainers-wish-you-knew.

89   Anne Truitt, *Daybook: The Journal of An Artist* (New York: Penguin Books, 1982), 140.

90   Jane McGonigal, *Superbetter: A Revolutionary Approach to Getting Stronger, Happier, Braver, and More Resilient* (New York: Penguin Press, 2015), 176.

91 Julia Cameron, *Walking in This World: The Practical Art of Creativity* (New York: Tarcher Press, 2003), 10.

92 James Clear, "Make More Art: The Benefits of Creativity," *Huffington Post*, December 23, 2015, https://www.huffpost.com/entry/make-more-art-the-health-benefits-of-creativity_n_8868802.

93 Megan Gannon, "I Can Haz Productivity? Why You Should Look at Cute Animals at Work," *Live Science* (blog), September 27, 2012, https://www.livescience.com/23515-cute-animal-images-boost-work-performance.html.

94 Renée van der Vennet & Susan Serice (2012) "Can Coloring Mandalas Reduce Anxiety? A Replication Study," *Art Therapy*, 29:2, 8792, https://doi.org/10.1080/07421656.2012.680047

95 Emma Seppala, "Connectedness and Health: The Science of Social Connection," *Stanford Medicine: The Center for Compassion and Altruism Research and Education*, May 9, 2014, http://ccare.stanford.edu/uncategorized/connectedness-health-the-science-of-social-connection-infographic/.

96 Tom Jacobs, "Dim Lighting Sparks Creativity," *Pacific Standard*, June 18, 2013, https://psmag.com/economics/dim-lighting-sparks-creativity-60437.

97 Janice Wood, "Students Who Drink Water During Exams Get Higher Grades," *PsychCentral*, April 21, 2012, https://psychcentral.com/news/2012/04/21/students-who-drink-water-during-exams-get-higher-grades/37675.html.

98 Eleni Gage, "25 Easy Instant Energy Boosters," *Real Simple*, https://www.realsimple.com/health/mind-mood/emotional-health/easy-instant-energy-boosters?slide=58701#58701.

99 Eric Barker, "New Neuroscience Reveals 4 Rituals That Will Make You Happy," *Barking Up the Wrong Tree* (blog), September 2015, https://www.bakadesuyo.com/2015/09/make-you-happy-2/.

100 Nina Elias, "Why Your Brain Games Aren't Working," *Prevention*, October 29, 2013, https://www.prevention.com/life/a20461776/research-shows-crosswords-not-enough-for-brain-boosting/.

101 Lea Winerman, "A Messy Desk Encourages a Creative Mind, Study Finds," *APA Monitor on Psychology*, October 2013, https://www.apa.org/monitor/2013/10/messy-desk.

102 Douglas LaBier, "How Music Improves Your Mood and Outlook on Life," *Progressive Impact* (blog), May 17, 2013, https://www.progressiveimpact.org/how-music-improves-your-mood-and-outlook-on-life/.

103 Tony Schwartz and Jim Loehr, *The Power of Full Engagement: Managing Energy, Not Time, Is the Key to High Performance and Personal Renewal* (New York: Free Press, 2003), 61.

104 Lizzie Streit, "Coffee Nap: Can Caffeine Before a Nap Boost Energy Levels," *HealthLine* (blog), September 6, 2018, https://www.healthline.com/nutrition/coffee-nap.

105 Fred Bryant and Joseph Veroff, *Savoring: A New Model of Positive Experience* (London: Psychology Press, 2006).

106 "11 Surprising Health Benefits of Singing," *Take Lessons* (blog), https://take-lessons.com/live/singing/health-benefits-of-singing.

107 Kristen Morales, "Skip the Caffeine, Opt for the Stairs to Feel More Ener-

gized," *UGA Today*, April 19 2017, https://news.uga.edu/stairs-more-ener-gy-research/.

108 "How to Savor," *The Positive Psychlopedia* (blog), https://positivepsychlopedia.com/year-of-happy/how-to-savor/.

109 Diana Yates, "Attention, Couch Potatoes! Walking Boosts Brain Connectivity, Function," *Illinois News Bureau*, August 26, 2010, https://news.illinois.edu/view/6367/205556.

110 "Taking a Walk May Lead to More Creativity than Sitting," *Science Daily*, April 24, 2014, https://www.sciencedaily.com/releases/2014/04/140424101556.htm.

111 Stephen Kaplan, "The Restorative Benefits of Nature: Toward an Integrative Framework," Journal of Environmental Psychology, Volume 15, Issue 3, September 1995, 169-182.

LEVEL UP INDEX

This index refers to quest numbers.

ACKNOWLEDGEMENTS

I'm grateful every day for the privilege of working as a writer, coach, and artist educator.

I'm deeply grateful for you, my coaches, mentors, teachers, friends, and family, for supporting me in this journey. I couldn't have done it without you. If your name doesn't appear here, and it should, that's on me for being a "cotton-headed ninny-muggins." (Thanks to the movie *Elf* for that expression).

A heartfelt thank you to my coach, George Kao, and the MasterHeart coaching group: your presence and support means the world to me.

I appreciate all of my writing buddies and critique partners. You nudge and encourage me to keep writing and do it better: Jocelyn Kohler, Sharon Nagel, Marybeth Shaffer, Jeanette Hurt, Margaret Rode, Jane Rubietta, Jeannée Sacken, Jane Young, Sandy Brehl, Jerrianne Hayslett, Christa von Zychlin, Deanna Singh, and Kira Bigwood.

My badass friends Melissa Dorn, Juliet Droege, and Karen Natterstad regularly encourage me to face my fear and do it anyway. Thank you all for cheering me on.

A huge thank you to all of the other badass friends, librarians, teachers, coaches, and therapists in my life. You rock.

Thanks to the Milwaukee Public Library and Arts@Large for supporting Dream Keepers and my work as an artist educator. And a huge, humble burst of gratitude to all of the young people who have opened up their hearts and told their stories.

So many people work to make a book readable for you. I'm grateful to Amanda Valentine for her keen eye and gaming know-how: you made this book better. Thomas Deeny created the beautiful layout for the book. And thanks to James from GoOnWrite.com for the amazing cover design.

Most of all, much love and gratitude to my family. You put up with my late nights and long weekends, pulling me out of my office to take walks, watch movies, and go to plays. My sweet and loving husband, Harold Eppley, listened to me whine, helped with last-minute text tasks, and cooked me delicious meals. My children, Sam and Eliana, made me laugh and reminded me to stop worrying. You keep me grounded—and I am so grateful for you all.

ABOUT THE AUTHOR

Write Now! Coach Rochelle Melander is a certified professional coach, experienced publishing strategist, and artist educator. She is the author of eleven books, including *Write-A-Thon: Write Your Book in 26 Days (And Live to Tell About It)*. Write Now! Coach provides solutions for people who feel stuck, overwhelmed or confused by the writing and publishing process. She is the founder of Dream Keepers, a writing workshop that supports children and teens in finding their voice and sharing their stories. Visit her online to learn more, sign up for Write Now! Tips, or book a consultation: https://writenowcoach.com/

CPSIA information can be obtained
at www.ICGtesting.com
Printed in the USA
LVHW020159180619
621463LV00020B/856